MW00681137

E L E V A T E

Take Your Business to the Next Level

John,

Elevate to new levels!

E. Jr

ERIK THERWANGER

ELEVATE

Take Your Business to the Next Level

The Think**GREAT**®
COLLECTION

Published in Prior Lake, Minnesota, by Think GREAT® LLC

ELEVATE™ is a trademark of Think GREAT® LLC

Think GREAT® is a registered trademark of Think GREAT® LLC

ISBN 978-0-9909039-5-6

Library of Congress Subject Headings:

Business & Economics / Strategic Planning

BISAC Subject Headings:

BUS063000   Business & Economics / Strategic Planning

ELEVATE_Book_v23CS1 – 07-01-2016

Dedication

This book is dedicated to every business owner, entre-
prenuer, and leader who has the vision and drive for
reaching new levels of success. Your desire to elevate the
performance of your team and the results of your organization, will lead the way to new, exciting, and life-changing
destinations.

To my clients, who have opened up their businesses and
their hearts to me, sharing their dreams of elevating to
new levels. It is a privilege to be your Business Flight Instructor.

Contents

Introduction

Are You Ready for Take Off?

Your Business Was Not Designed to Stay on the Ground.

"Yuma Ground, this is Top Gun One-Five, ready for taxi." That was the first sound I heard as I put my headset on in the control tower at Marine Corps Air Station, Yuma, Arizona. I was eighteen years old and had just completed four months of intense air traffic control (ATC) school at the Naval Air Station in Millington, Tennessee.

As a young U.S. Marine, I was anxious to return the proper command to the pilot in the F-14 Tomcat, a high-powered fighter aircraft. Yes, just like the ones in the movie, *Top Gun*. Under the watchful eye of the corporal training me, I responded, "Top Gun One-Five, Yuma Ground, taxi to Runway Two-One, caution the C-130 on your left."

The ATC tower stretched ten stories into the sky, providing air traffic controllers a vantage point, from which we could see clearly for miles. High above the airfield, I looked down and watched the plane begin to roll forward. As the pilot guided his aircraft, moving closer to the runway, my excitement level grew. Top Gun One-Five slowed and stopped, just short of entering Runway Two-One.

Switching radio frequency to Local Control, the pilot was now speaking to the gunnery sergeant standing next to me. Issuing the command to enter the runway, the F-14 slowly positioned itself, turning to face the opposite end, three miles away. The naval officer, piloting this aircraft, was about to operate this vehicle with its most simple function... to fly.

Without the ability to perform this one basic task, the aircraft was essentially useless, unable to complete even the smallest mission. The moment was now here and the command from local control was given. "Top Gun One-Five, you are cleared for take-off." With those ten simple words, the engines revved higher and the plane accelerated. Momentum rapidly increased as the jet blast poured from the engines. The F-14 was quickly speeding forward at over 100 mph.

Within seconds, the front wheels lifted off of the runway. The nose of the aircraft angled up and then the rear wheels left the ground. Seconds later, Top Gun One-Five was nearly one thousand feet in the air. With a few final adjustments, the pilot turned his plane toward the vast Yuma Desert and disappeared into the horizon.

Like this aircraft, your business was never intended to stay on the ground, aimlessly taxiing around, or worse yet, stuck motionless in a hanger. But that is how many business leaders feel - grounded. You know your business is capable of achieving higher levels of success. But are you prepared to reach them?

POSITION YOUR BUSINESS FOR SUCCESS

You have opened the pages of this book for one reason. You are ready to elevate the performance of your team and the results of your organization. If you are prepared to take your business to new levels, you must develop your skills and become the business pilot your aircraft needs.

Imagine what it will feel like to transform your organization into a high-performance aircraft. Imagine the feeling of building a laser-focused crew, capable of accomplishing any mission. Now, imagine what it will feel like as you put on your flight suit, power up your well-oiled machine, and take off to the levels of success you have only dreamed of.

In many cases, your business has already achieved some levels of growth. But too often, you may have experienced the feelings of worry, fear, or frustrations as your aircraft struggles to get off the ground, let alone, to achieve and maintain your desired "flight" levels. It can be immensely discouraging to lose altitude; not only for you, but for your team.

Striving for growth can present new challenges, but no challenge is more threatening than the reality of staying grounded, especially while other aircraft are taking off around you. That feeling can now be a thing of the past. *ELEVATE* is much more than a collection of proven, real-world experiences, it is your navigation system, air traffic control support, and maintenance procedures, all rolled into one powerfully focused system:

The Business Elevation System (BES).

As an air traffic controller, I was trained to direct air traffic, and never experienced the adrenaline rush of piloting a plane. As a business coach, however, I now apply my ATC experiences in the corporate world.

A NEW DESTINATION

After serving in the Marine Corps, I used my G.I. Bill and pursued a career in the entertainment industry. I attended Orange Coast College, in Costa Mesa, California (Go Pirates!) then was accepted to the film school at the University of Southern California (Fight On Trojans!).

In the early 2000s, I interviewed for a position at a media company in Santa Monica, California. It was a small business, with a dozen employees, specializing in editorial services, video duplication, and DVD replication. They produced broadcast quality video elements for companies such as MTV, HBO, and Comedy Central.

During my interview, I spoke directly with the owner about his goals. He purchased the company about eight years prior and had experienced some growth, but not at the consistent rate he wanted. He knew that his company was capable of more, but felt grounded: trapped on the airfield when he should be soaring in the skies, high above.

By this point in my career, I not only had experience in the entertainment industry, but I also had strong sales skills, and the leadership traits I developed in the U.S. Marine Corps. The owner felt that his company was performing at about half of its potential and dreamed of elevating to a level of doubling their annual sales. But he was unsure of where to start.

Like most business owners, he was more than willing to work "in" the mechanics of his business, wearing many of the hats that his crew should have been wearing. But, this prevented him from piloting his plane and working "on" the elevation of his business. Sound familiar?

Business pilots who lack the opportunity to fly their planes are left feeling overwhelmed and trapped in their own immobile aircrafts. At the time of my interview, only an entry-level position was available. But the owner's passion for his company, and belief in my skills, encouraged me to take the opportunity and utilize my experiences to help his company to grow.

As the results grew, he reassured me that my career would too. With a tour of his facility and a solid handshake, I joined his team. We began to map out the enhancements necessary to allow his aircraft to achieve consistently high levels of success.

By applying the concepts in this book, we not only took off, but we climbed well past the goal of doubling annual sales. Within five years, our annual sales grew by more than 300%, our margins increased, and we nearly eliminated all internal errors. Most importantly, we developed a crew of leaders and impacted our team and clients in significantly positive ways.

Sounds simple, doesn't it? The good news is that it is simple. Not easy, but simple. You already have what it takes to put in the hard work, dedication, and passion necessary for growth. Now, you can step back into the cockpit and elevate your business.

ELEVATE

It can seem like a daunting task to get something to take flight. Business pilots often feel overwhelmed at the thought of getting their planes in the air, and keeping them there. Are you tired of wondering what the view looks like from the heavens? Then now is the time to ELEVATE.

As an air traffic controller, I had the privilege of seeing nearly every type of military and civilian aircraft take off from MCAS, Yuma. But one in particular always fascinated me. On occasion, the Air Force would fly in their huge C-5s. Designed for cargo transportation, this aircraft is 247 feet long and has a fully loaded weight of 769,000 lbs. That's over 380 tons.

It is almost incomprehensible to think that this huge piece of metal can get off the ground. But it does. While transporting tanks, other aircraft, supplies, and scores of troops, this beast of a plane can fly at heights of

35,000 feet. That is seven miles up. How can it elevate, you ask? Because it follows the same basic aviation principles that all other aircraft use.

The Four Forces of Flight:

1. Thrust

2. Drag

3. Lift

4. Weight

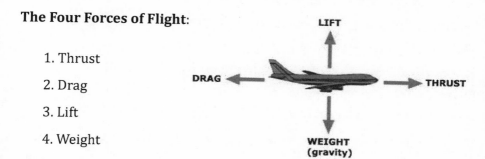

Without getting too detailed into the physics of sustainable flight, each aircraft encounters these four forces, and the pilot must achieve the proper balance between them to take off and maintain elevation. Most importantly, flying conditions are not always ideal, so pilots must be prepared to handle the less-than-adequate circumstances they will face.

As a business pilot, you may feel that your business is like a heavy C-5, so weighted down with extra cargo, that it would be impossible to take off. The *Business Elevation System* will allow you to move beyond the fear of the dreaded "crash and burn" and experience consistent elevation.

ELEVATE introduces you to the principles required for business flight, providing you with the balance required for new levels of growth, regardless of the obstacles you encounter. Like a flight instructor, I teach business pilots to balance the components necessary for business elevation.

The Four Forces of Business Elevation:

1. Flight Plan Creation

2. Aircrew Development

3. Tactical Maneuvers

4. Ascension Enhancement

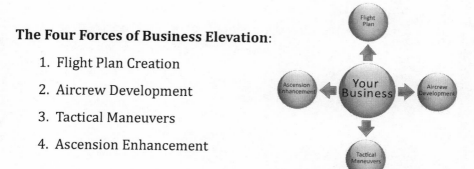

As an active corporate coach, I work directly with my clients and their teams, sharing the principles of *ELEVATE*. My core client is typically a small to medium business, ranging from $1,000,000 to $25,000,000 in annual revenue and often having teams from ten to fifty employees.

My larger, Fortune 500 level clients have most of their systems and processes already established, but the foundational components of *ELEVATE* allows their leaders to empower their teams and their departments, further elevating the success of their entire organization.

By adopting the strategies and techniques of the *Business Elevation System*, business pilots are able to guide their aircraft to new heights, shifting their efforts from working "in" their businesses, to working "on" them.

How do you know if *ELEVATE* is right for you? That's a GREAT question. Whether a business is small or large, publicly held or privately owned, GREAT Business Pilots have three things in common.

The 3 Characteristics of GREAT Business Pilots:

1. **Committed** to achieving greater results

2. **Open** for new, dynamic ideas

3. **Ready** to take immediate action

If this describes you, then you can become the business pilot who positions your company for success; the business pilot who allows your organization to *ELEVATE* to new levels.

Before turning the page, I want you think for a moment about the dream company you desire. Let the excitement of seeing your business rise into the skies fill your mind and fuel your spirit. Let these thoughts be the beacon of positivity that will guide you and your crew to new destinations.

Think GREAT,

Erik

Pre-Flight Briefing

The Business Elevation System

(BES)

Once you have tasted flight, you will forever walk the earth with your eyes turned skyward, for there you have been, and there you will always long to return.

~ Leonardo da Vinci

Pre-Flight Briefing

The Business Elevation System (BES)

Upgrading Your Business Aircraft.

Each year, military airfields open their gates, allowing millions of civilians to attend their annual air shows. Packed with people anxious to see all of the amazing aircraft in our nation's fleet, these events are filled with excitement and awe.

It was the summer of 1991, just shortly before I completed my tour of duty, when I attended the air show at Marine Corps Air Station El Toro, in Southern California. It was estimated that 500,000 people visited the base over the weekend to catch a glimpse of our country's military aircraft.

The airfield was covered with virtually every type of plan and helicopter. Old bi-planes from WWI, B-2 Bombers from WWII, and the current fighter and attack aircraft used in Desert Storm were all on display.

Children ran around the planes, while their parents took a closer look at all of the high-tech controls, cargo bays, and weapons mounted on each aircraft. But perhaps my favorite part of the entire air show was the conversations I heard from older veterans as they shared stories of their combat experiences in these planes.

To say that there were high levels of excitement would be an understatement. The voices of hundreds of thousands of people filled the air, until they were loudly interrupted by the deafening burst of the Blue Angels flying overhead. Like an explosion of thunder, the air show officially began, as the blue and yellow jets flew a few hundred feet above the airfield.

In perfect synchronization, the five F-18s performed aviation maneuvers that captivated the entire audience. With their wings merely feet apart, the pilots moved as a unit, showcasing their skills and our military might. The sounds of applause and cheering nearly drowned out their engines.

As the Blue Angles performed their final maneuvers, they made one last pass over the airfield then disappeared into the skies. Once out of sight, people re-focused their attention back to the planes on the ground. I made an interesting observation that day as each of the performing aircraft completed their routines and flew into the distance.

While each guest enjoyed seeing the planes parked on the airfield, the greatest excitement, energy, and enthusiasm came from observing them in the sky; watching them do what they were designed for. Does your business create that level of excitement and engagement in your team? In you?

It was a huge undertaking to put together an air show of this size. Hundreds of pilots participated that day to make it a special event. But they were not alone. They were part of a team, utilizing a system to achieve the desired levels of elevation and success.

What the audience did not see, was the massive amount of detailed planning that went into this event the year leading up to it. In addition to the pre-flight briefings, which kept everyone on the same page that day, the air show consisted of many moving parts and key personnel. The pilots were the heroes of the day, but they never flew without a crew.

Other critical factors come into play: safety precautions, emergency extraction plans, weather conditions, support staff, logistics, marketing, advertising, and promotions. Not a single pilot just jumped into the pilot's seat and decided to go fly that day. But some business pilots attempt to do that with their businesses and wonder why things go wrong.

Successful pilots have more than a plan. They have a detailed system, designed with everything needed for a safe flight and mission accomplishment. To create the excitement and awe you desire, as your business elevates, you will need a system; a system that will remove the guess work, unify your crew, and help you to reach new heights.

THE BUSINESS ELEVATION SYSTEM - BES

The success of your business is far too important to leave things to chance; to literally wing-it. The *Business Elevation System* does more than put you back in the pilot's seat, it teaches you how to take control of the four elements required for business elevation, and make the necessary maneuvers that a growing business requires.

YOUR GUIDE TO SUCCESSFUL FLIGHT

ELEVATE is your business flight school. Divided into four powerful sections, you will have a step-by-step guide to mastering each element of a successful business flight.

Part 1: Flight Plan Creation

Learn how to transform your dreams and vision into an empowering **Destination**, inspiring your entire crew. Design a crystal-clear **Route** that outlines the exact steps, and the course-correction necessary for success. Take control of time as you set the **ETA**, creating a sense of urgency to ensure mission accomplishment.

Part 2: Aircrew Development

The success of every flight is determined largely by the entire crew. Position **Business Aviators** to fly your aircraft, while developing and enhancing the skills of the **Business Flight Crew**. Also, identify and utilize the power of **Business Synergy**. Together, your entire team will help your business aircraft to take off and climb to new heights.

Part 3: Tactical Maneuvers

Every flight encounters challenges and yours will be no different. Navigating around the **Obstacles** and maneuvering through the **Turbulence** will ensure a successful flight. By focusing on improving communication, you will continually guard against the dangers of flight hazards.

Part 4: Ascension Enhancement

Getting your business in the air is important, but staying there is critical. You will keep your aircraft soaring as you learn the techniques of improving your **Structural Integrity** while understanding how to perform **In-Flight Refueling**. Most importantly, you will simultaneously be climbing to new levels as you and your crew **Earn Your Flight Wings** and reach unexpected levels of growth and success.

The real-world concepts and applications in *ELEVATE* allowed us to grow the media company by over 300% and has positioned me to support thousands of business leaders in the elevation of their companies. But what separates *ELEVATE* from other business "How To" books and programs?

Unique to *ELEVATE*, I intertwine my specialized leadership experiences from the Marine Corps to help business pilots to further strengthen their system... to ascend higher. By implementing a foundation of leadership development, companies enhance morale, improve customer satisfaction, increase referrals, and prepare their teams for higher levels of performance. Leadership fuels elevation.

Throughout the pages of *ELEVATE*, you will also encounter powerful entries from the *Pilot's Log*, just like the one below. These tips, strategies, and techniques will further enhance your flight experience.

Pilot's Log:
The foundation of business elevation is leadership development - for your entire team.

90-DAY FLIGHT

One of the common themes, linking all six of my books together, is the concept that human beings have the unique ability to stay focused on important goals for about 90 days. There are multitudes of 90-day and 12-week programs to help people improve their personal and professional lives.

During Marine Corps Boot Camp, I experienced 90 days of intense training and development with the other young recruits. But at the end, the men of Platoon 1095 had been transformed from civilians to Marines.

I use a 90-Day Run in my book, *The GOAL Formula*, as a tool to help people transform goals into realities. I also use it as a sales tool in my book, *3-D Sales*, to increase sales results. In *The LEADERSHIP Connection*, I show leaders how to use this concept to collapse time frames on success.

As the vice president of the media company, I constantly launched back-to-back 90-Day Runs to enhance our performance, and accomplish, then exceed the goals we set.

ELEVATE allows you and your crew to embark on a 90-Day Flight, achieving the objectives necessary to stay on track with your mission. Like most aircraft, your business probably does not require a major engine overhaul to increase performance. Some well-placed, well-timed carburetor adjustments will typically allow most companies to experience elevation.

BUSINESS-FLIGHT CHECKLIST

If you were about to pilot an aircraft, how important would a checklist be to you, to ensure a safe and successful flight? It would be of the highest importance. The Federal Aviation Administration's (FAA) practical test standards clearly state that pilots must use appropriate written checklists prior to flight. Every pilot understands and values their importance.

Failure to utilize this tool can yield dire results to an aircraft and its crew, or to a business and its team. While there are hundreds of items that a pilot could check before a flight, some of the common ones are:

- ☐ Auxiliary Fuel Pump
- ☐ Instruments/Radios
- ☐ Altimeter
- ☐ Fuel Gauges
- ☐ Flight Controls
- ☐ Seat Belts
- ☐ Directional Gyro
- ☐ Parking Brake

If you're like me, these sound extremely important and I certainly appreciate a pilot who takes the time to put these items as a priority when I fly. Your *Pre-Flight Checklist* is equally important, but many business pilots try to take off and accomplish their missions with very little preventative assessment.

As a business pilot, there are items you should identify, and adjust, fix, or create prior to take off. For the good of your business, your team and your success, always start with your *Pre-Flight Checklist* (page 7).

ELEVATE
Pre-Flight Checklist

Gauge the status of your aircraft before attempting to fly. Rank each, on a scale of 1-10, 10 being best.

Our leadership team is in place	1 2 3 4 5 6 7 8 9 10
Our entire team is fully engaged	1 2 3 4 5 6 7 8 9 10
Team Identity is established	1 2 3 4 5 6 7 8 9 10
We have a unifying Culture	1 2 3 4 5 6 7 8 9 10
Customer/Clients are satisfied	1 2 3 4 5 6 7 8 9 10
Sales Performance is rising	1 2 3 4 5 6 7 8 9 10
Our Marketing Plan is solid	1 2 3 4 5 6 7 8 9 10
We have established important Goals	1 2 3 4 5 6 7 8 9 10
We have a 3-5 Year Strategic Plan	1 2 3 4 5 6 7 8 9 10
We have a 1 Year Tactical Plan	1 2 3 4 5 6 7 8 9 10
Each upcoming quarter is planned	1 2 3 4 5 6 7 8 9 10
Our next 90 days are mapped out	1 2 3 4 5 6 7 8 9 10

Part I

Flight Plan Creation

A mile of highway will take you just one mile, but a mile of runway will take you anywhere.

~ Anonymous

Part I

Flight Plan Creation

Where do you want to go?

My corporate coaching duties position me in front of many business pilots who aimlessly wander around the airfield of mediocrity. With the best of intentions, they taxi around, gaining some momentum then losing it. Refocusing their efforts and trying to rekindle their passion, they gain momentum again. But quickly lose it. And the cycle continues.

No matter what they attempt, no matter what direction they point their aircraft, they go nowhere. Some bravely roll back onto the runway, move their aircraft forward, then exit a taxiway before attempting a take off. They often abandon their pilot's seat and find themselves caught up in the minutia of maintaining and running their aircraft - not flying it.

With the hopes of elevation, these dedicated business pilots occasionally stop to survey their planes and assess their crews, momentarily wondering if their organization is still capable of flight. Is it possible to elevate a business that is currently grounded, or perhaps has been immobile for long periods of time? Yes, it 100% is.

The owner of the media company had a simple goal: double sales. Was his company capable of achieving this high level of elevation? He felt it was. Did he have passion? Yes. Did he have desire? Most certainly. Did he possess a strong belief level in himself and his company? Absolutely! So why was his business still on the ground?

Let's ask a better question. Did he have a plan? No, he did not. Essentially, he was accomplishing exactly what was in his plan... nothing. Without a plan, his goals, his passion, his desire, and even his belief level remained on the airfield. Elevation is not possible without a solid plan.

The unfortunate fact is that most business pilots do not have a working flight plan. "Working," as in promoting action. When I first meet with these pilots, I strive to gain a better understanding of their businesses. With great pride, they share their amazing goals: increased sales, high levels of morale, satisfied customers, engaged team members, and dozens of other remarkable objectives.

With such empowering goals, I excitedly ask to see their plan for transforming their dreams into realities. That question is typically met with a somber look on their faces that says to me, "I need help." With their planes indefinitely stranded on the ground, I quickly discover one of the missing forces of business flight. They have a lackluster plan, or worse yet, no plan at all.

"We are planning to put together a plan," "We talked about that," or, "We're working on that," are common responses. But most business pilots inevitably admit, "We don't have one." Now, you can have a flight plan that allows your team to understand your destination and prepare for elevation.

AVIATION FLIGHT PLAN

With lives on the line for every flight, it would be easy to imagine that an aviation flight plan would be a complex document, accounting for many variables. To the contrary. Because detailed systems are in place and proper communication is established, the flight plan is actually a simple set of key elements, providing the essential information required for successfully launching and tracking thousands of flights each day.

A properly completed flight plan is often a small sheet of paper, filed prior to departure. These "Air Maps" allow pilots to communicate their intentions with their crew, air traffic controllers, and other airfield support staff. Yes, every flight has a plan because every flight is that important.

Flight plans include vital information such as departure and arrival points, estimated time en route, and alternate airports in case of hazards. They are especially critical when navigating over inhospitable areas, such as large bodies of water, or vast deserts. If a flight is overdue, the flight plan is a fast way of alerting rescuers of a possible emergency situation.

A flight plan sounds simple because it is. Your business flight plan needs to be simple, too. I have seen business plans the size of encyclopedias, costing tens of thousands of dollars to develop. Though they are impressive documents, those businesses still remain on the ground, and their pilots remain frustrated and exhausted.

Throwing money at a plan does not guarantee its success. *ELEVATE* will position you to create a flight plan with your leadership team, breathing life into both your plan and your organization. After all, the main purpose of a plan is to inspire action, and every internal component of that plan should support and serve that key objective.

THE LEADER'S ROLE

Complicated plans seldom work. That is why leaders take the complex and make it simple, empowering their entire teams to take the actions necessary for elevation. Why else would you invest the time and resources in developing a plan? To keep it on a shelf, collecting dust? Absolutely not!

The role of a leader cannot be understated in the success of the *Business Elevation System*. The *BES* is not designed to achieve movement without purpose; it was developed to achieve GREAT levels of elevation. The success of your plan will rest on the shoulders of the leaders who create and implement it.

Pilot's Log:
A strong leader will do more with a weak plan than a weak leader ever can do with a strong plan.

For a Business Flight Plan to succeed, business pilots must take a leadership role within their organizations. When something is important, you must lead, and your flight plan is critically important. You will not *manage* your way to your destination. But business executives routinely confuse management and leadership, using the terms interchangeably, much to their detriment.

To achieve elevation, a clear distinction between management and leadership must be made. Fortunately, that distinction is simple:

> ## *Manage the Work - Lead the People.*

As air traffic controllers, the Marine Corps taught us to manage the work; the planes taking off and landing each day. I may have been trained as an air traffic controller, but I was developed as a leader. As a corporal, I learned to lead Marines, inspiring and encouraging them to perform at the highest levels of excellence.

You and your crew will manage the components of your plan (goals, objectives, and processes). But you will be best served to apply the traits and principles of leadership to your crew (guiding, mentoring, and coaching).

Pilot's Log:
Leaders make an impact, leaving a lasting impression in the lives of everyone they encounter.

For more detailed concepts, strategies, and techniques on leading your team to success, check out my book, *The LEADERSHIP Connection.*

A SIMPLE PLAN

As leaders, we accomplish things through the efforts of others. That includes the goals and objectives detailed in our flight plans. So it is in our best interest to simplify everything. If we expect our people to follow us, and support our plans, we must be able to answer the three key questions they will ask, or they will inevitably be thinking about.

By investing the time to provide the right answers to these questions, you will help to ensure organizational success, team engagement, and business elevation. This is the first step back into the cockpit.

The Three Key Questions of a Flight Plan:

- Where are we going?

- How do we get there?

- When will we arrive?

Well, that was simple. Your Business Flight Plan is a guide, allowing you to map out your trip from *Point A to Point B*, and highlighting the necessary steps on everything in between. Answering these three key questions, while providing the mechanisms for tracking your progress, will bring your destination into clear view, for you and your team.

For many business pilots, the planning process undoubtedly can seem daunting, intimidating, and time consuming. When you factor in all of the hats we wear and all of the fires we are constantly putting out, the idea of finding the time to create a plan can seem like wishful thinking.

The next three chapters will allow you and your leaders to create your flight plan by providing the answers to the three key questions:

The Three Key Answers of a Flight Plan:

- Destination - Where we are going?

- Route   - How we are getting there?

- ETA   - When we will arrive?

This is an exciting time as you and your leaders envision your destination, design your route, and establish the time frames required for success. Your Flight Plan will combine specific elements that will not only provide you and your team with the right answers, but will position your organization with the main focus: to *ELEVATE*.

Suit up! It's time to report to base operations. You are about to create your Business Flight Plan.

Chapter 1

Your Destination

Moving Your Team to a Dynamic Location.

There is no answer more deflating than, "I don't know," especially when the question is, "Where are we going?" As a leader, it is safe to say that you want your people to follow you. Put yourself in their shoes for a moment. If someone asked you to follow them, or merely implied that you should follow them, what would your first question be? "Where are we going?"

That is exactly what your team is thinking every time you expect them to follow your lead. They are contemplating that question while you are pondering why no one is following you. If you feel like you are on a walk by yourself, stop asking, "Why are they not following me?" and start asking, "Where am I leading them?"

Only *Your Destination* will answer this question. Have you provided your team with a specific destination, one that excites and empowers? Have you shared a destination that encourages movement? Without movement, no one can follow you.

In today's quick-fix culture, leaders are often led to believe that vision is everything, and that sharing their vision is a fix-all for their businesses. Vision is in fact one thing; not everything. Even a strong vision will ultimately lose its power to *move* people without the identification of a dynamic destination.

Should a leader have vision? Absolutely. But it is often incorrectly assumed that most entrepreneurs, business owners, and executive leaders possess a powerful, detailed vision for their company. Most do not. Instead, they typically have high levels of passion, energy, and enthusiasm. All are needed for elevation, but more is required.

They believe in the amazing capabilities of their aircraft, but they are unfortunately unable to clearly articulate this into empowering messages for themselves and their crew. These messages are essential tools needed for a successful flight plan; the exact tools needed for high levels of elevation.

When a leader only shares vision, but takes no steps in the direction to a destination, the team loses faith in that leader, no matter how strong that particular message is. Vision, without a specified destination, is merely an image in the head of the person who created it. Your Business Flight Plan will help you to establish much more than just your vision.

Successful business pilots transform their vision, mission, core values, and goals into a destination that their crews believe in. These components create additional buy-in as they are shared regularly with team members. Your destination should empower, entice, and encourage your team to follow you, while simultaneously creating two powerful components necessary for elevation: engagement and identity.

Pilot's Log:
Leaders not only establish a destination, they constantly share their emowering messages with their teams.

ELEVATE ENGAGEMENT

A destination provides much more to your team than just answering the question, "Where are we going?" The answer engages them, and engagement is critically important for elevation. How important? Recent polls suggest that nearly 75% of employees are disengaged. Are three out of four of your team members disengaged? Can you expect to elevate with only 25% of your crew fully supporting your efforts? Not hardly.

Worse yet, these polls state that nearly 20% of employees actively try to undermine engaged team members. Are one out of five of your team members undermining the efforts of their co-workers? What is the likelihood of your aircraft taking off, and elevating to high levels, with a disengaged team?

Imagine sitting in a plane and having the flight attendant start her safety message with, "Welcome aboard: 72% of our crew are disengaged while 18% are actively undermining the rest of our crew. Have a nice flight." It does not make any sense, does it? But everyday, business pilots face this aeronautical nightmare.

The end result? They fail to get even the front wheels of their plane off the ground and the business pilot is left feeling discouraged, while the crew witnesses yet another failed attempt. Which, by the way, reaffirms their disengagement in the first place.

To say that you need an engaged crew to elevate is an understatement. Because you cannot elevate alone, you cannot afford to lose the war on disengagement in your organization. Elevation is a team endeavor and successful leaders do not take the concept of team engagement lightly. Engaged team members will be the first to start following you.

The polls did have a positive report on the results of engagement. Engaged team members tend to be over 30% more productive than their disengaged counterparts, and engaged sales people produce over 35% greater results. It pays to create engagement.

ELEVATE IDENTITY

People want to be part of something special; something GREAT. Your Business Flight Plan will create more engagement by developing and enhancing your team's identity. Each component of your plan serves specific purposes, and the first six sections will begin to build a team identity, unifying your crew and creating the additional buy-in necessary for a successful flight.

I never assume anything when helping a company to elevate. Working with my clients, I am amazed at how many of their crew members do not fully understand the aircraft they are working "in." Note, I did not say working "on" because "on" implies striving for growth (elevation). If you do not understand the full capabilities of the organization, it is safe to say that you cannot unleash its true potential.

The first step to creating the Business Flight Plan is to complete the six steps toward the exciting process of determining a destination (page 26 and 27). Sometimes the following information is in place. If it is, you are off to a faster start. If it is not, you have a starting point. Current information, which does not support your destination, must be enhanced.

6 Components of Business Identity:

- *Company Name & Tagline*
- *History*
- *Capabilities*
- *Mission*
- *Vision*
- *Core Values*

Company Name & Tagline:

This is an easy first step. Jot down your company name. Underneath it, list your tagline. What's a tagline, you ask? It's your slogan. Taglines are not used by every organization, but can immensely help to increase identity.

The Few, the Proud, the Marines. This slogan is much more than the six words you just read. For Marines, it is our identity, representing the deep commitment level of all members. It emphasizes that we are part of something special, and allows us to elevate each time our nation calls on us.

A tagline can be the single-most dynamic, powerful expression of your brand, implying a promise to your team and customers. It is a key indicator of the future experience in working for and with your organization. At the media company, our tagline was, "Your One-Stop Media Shop." This announced to our clients (and team) that we were more than just a single media service. We offered much more and we wanted everyone to know.

Creating, or enhancing your tagline, does not require high levels of creativity, but rather, high levels of truth and honesty. More than clever wordsmithing, your tagline is your unique business signature, in one short sentence. It begins to unify your crew.

History:

To be a Marine of the future, we learned about the Marines of the past. A high reverence of our heritage further cemented our identity as we were taught about the birth of the Marine Corps, our battles and victories, and other key accomplishments that shaped us as an organization.

Understanding where you come from helps to understand where you are going: *Your Destination*. You can better plan for the future when you have a deeper understanding of your past. Your website and literature may already feature much of this information. But does it inspire your team?

Briefly describe your company's beginnings, milestones, and achievements to deepen the identity of your team.

Pilot's Log:
Be proud of your history.

Capabilities:

Describe what you do best; more than just your products and services.

I am often amazed, and a bit confused that most employees, and even many leaders, struggle to identify, and articulate, the core offerings of their company. Even sales people, within the same organization, describe their products and services differently. If your team has difficulty communicating your capabilities, how well do you expect your customers to understand them? Capabilities translate into identity.

Each aircraft in the military has specific capabilities, services if you will, that allow the pilots to accomplish their current missions. The functionality of military aircraft is so crucial that they are identified, alpha-numerically, to describe their expected capabilities.

Examples of some military aircraft designations:

A = Attack	*A-10, AV-8B, A-6*
B = Bomber	*B-1, B-2*
C = Cargo	*C-5, C-17, C-130*
F = Fighter	*F-14, F-16, F-18*
R = Reconnaissance	*SR-71, TR-1*

A deep understanding of your capabilities will empower your crew to feel confident in taking on new missions. Without this knowledge, the crew will be less likely to follow you; less enthusiastic to elevate.

In business, identifying your capabilities does more than list your core products and services. It positions you to share "why" you deliver them the way you do. Your competition has many of the same offerings, but your ability to identify your capabilities translates into greater customer satisfaction, team member engagement, and team identity.

Understanding our capabilities at the media company served a great purpose. We strove to position our clients for success by linking our products and services together. It was imperative that all of our team members knew exactly what we offered, so we could ensure that our customers understood exactly what we offered. If they don't know, you don't grow.

Here were our eight core services:

• *High Definition*	• *Editorial*
• *Duplication/Conversion*	• *Digital Restoration*
• *Data Services*	• *Replication*
• *DVD Mastering*	• *Language Services*

Your business capabilities describe "what" you do, not "how" you do it. Capabilities are not a processes. They are more than products and services; capabilities establish outcomes. Most importantly, they help to answer "why" you do "what" you do.

Our team deeply understood what we did, but they passionately shared why we did them. We collaborated and consulted with our clients, on all of their projects, while we collapsed time frames by getting things done right the first time. Our capabilities made us more relevant to our clients.

Mission:

There are thousands of ideas on what constitutes a mission statement. I believe that succinctly summarizing your business mission allows you to focus on the steps you need to move toward your destination. Your mission is your organization's current state: it's purpose, why it exists.

Your mission is where you are now. Describe what your company currently strives to do each day. At the media company, we collectively worked to define who we were. Once we had our mission statement, we were motivated to accomplish our mission. A mission statement creates movement.

Here was our Mission Statement from the media company:

> *Our mission is to be the finest quality provider of post production and media services.*
>
> *We will EXCEED our customers' expectations, by providing unparalleled customer service, while maintaining cutting-edge technology.*
>
> *We are dedicated to providing a culture with the opportunity for unlimited growth, and enrichment in the personal and professional lives of our team.*

This was created in 2004, but I just got inspired reading it again. Does your mission statement inspire you? Does it *move* your team?

Pilot's Log:

Your mission statement should reflect what makes your business and your team special and unique.

Vision:

Again, you will discover a multitude of philosophies on what a vision statement is, how to create it, and most importantly, why you should be sharing it on a regular basis. And you should.

Different than your mission, which is a snapshot of your company's current state, your vision is the future image of your business. Describe what your company is going to become, which will be the guiding light, allowing you and your crew to clearly see the path to your destination.

Here was our Vision Statement from the media company:

> ***Our vision is to lead the charge to search for and provide our clients with the greatest variety of media solutions – worldwide!***

Our vision statement had significantly less words than our mission statement, but so much more meaning. Not only did we surpass our flight level of 200% growth, but we elevated to over 300%. We arrived at significant destinations, including a second facility, while expanding our capabilities internationally into Europe. "Worldwide;" that one word meant so much to us. It enhanced our engagement and identity.

Your vision statement is an energizing component that will help to make your destination a reality. It is a brief, yet vivid description of the desired outcome of where you will be in the next three to five years, or beyond.

Work with your key leaders to summarize your vision with a powerful phrase that resonates with your entire crew, your customers, your vendors, and anyone who encounters your unique business aircraft.

Pilot's Log:
The *scope* of your vision statement is infinitely more important than the *size* of your vision statement.

YOUR DESTINATION | 25

Core Values:

Strengthen the foundation of your business by building your plan on the important, strong values that you and your team determine are relevant to your company. While "value" can often be linked to a monetary measure, true business value is defined as something else; something greater.

- Honor
- Courage
- Commitment

These three core values of the U.S. Marine Corps were chosen specifically to provide the bedrock of their character, the heart of their organization, and the spirit of their team.

Your core values are the unifying principles of your company that support your mission and vision. They further add to the identity of your team members and empower them to exemplify the highest levels of integrity, performance, and commitment.

Try to keep your list of core values to five or less. Having other values is important but your core values should promote an unrelenting determination to achieve a standard of excellence in every endeavor.

Below is a list of core values from other organizations. This can help you to pick the 3-5 core values that will elevate your team.

• *Achievement*	• *Enthusiasm*	• *Meaningful*
• *Adaptability*	• *Genuine*	• *Optimistic*
• *Belief*	• *Honesty*	• *Professional*
• *Compassion*	• *Innovation*	• *Resourceful*
• *Dedication*	• *Integrity*	• *Sincerity*

Your Core Values allow you and your crew to make better decisions in everything from hiring and selling, to building and elevating.

ELEVATE

90-Day FLIGHT PLAN

Company Name:

Tagline:

History:

Capabilities:

-
-

-
-

-
-

-
-

ELEVATE

90-Day FLIGHT PLAN

Mission:

Vision:

Core Values:

-
-
-
-
-

After completing the first six steps, you and your crew should be filled with the excitement of taking off and heading into the skies with your enhanced engagement and new-found identity.

The next step to creating the Business Flight Plan is to establish your flight levels, the goals necessary for success (page 34 and 35). Once your flight levels are established, you and your crew will strive to reach them.

Flight Levels - Your Business Goals:

- *High Flight Levels - Long-Term Goals*
  - *5 Year Goals*
  - *3 Year Goals*
  - *1 Year Goals*

- *Low Flight Levels - Short-Term Goals*
  - *Quarterly Goals*
  - *90 Day Goals*

LONG-TERM GOALS

To an Aviator, a flight level (FL) is specific altitude, measured in hundreds of feet. Flight level 250 (pronounced two-five-zero) translates to 25,000 feet above sea level. Flight level 300 equals 30,000 feet. Flying at such high levels serves a purpose for aircraft. The thinner air presents less drag, minimizing fuel consumption, and saving time and money.

To a business pilot, a flight level represents the goals necessary to arrive at their destination. Just like regular aircraft, not all business aircraft are capable of high flight levels. However, by setting and accomplishing important goals, businesses can scale up and create the ability to ascend higher.

You cannot accomplish your 5-year flight levels, without passing through your 3-year flight levels, 1-year flight levels, etc.

Long term goals are critically important to the growth of businesses and the well-being of their team members; perhaps more than most people understand. They guide our actions, which is what our plans are all about (taking action), and provide everyone with a sense of purpose. They keep people focused on maintaining high levels of positive, optimistic thoughts.

Once established, long-term goals and flight levels of great significance, remain in our subconscious mind. We cannot simply "erase" them. Failures, obstacles, and even negative people are incapable of stopping an important long-term goal, when the right leader is in the pilot's seat.

The Purpose of Long-Term Goals (High Flight Levels):

- Provide Direction
- Provide Meaning
- Provide Understanding

Provide Direction

Yogi Berra once said, "If you don't know where you are going, you'll end up someplace else." Having your high flight levels identified keeps your entire crew headed in the right direction. These long-term goals provide purpose and navigation for your short-term goals.

Provide Meaning

Going on a long trip can be exhausting, often challenging. Having powerful, long-term goals will bring a deeper meaning to every task and objective required for success. Goals without meaning mean nothing.

Provide Understanding

With a clear understanding of the long-range destination, you and your crew will be more prepared for the journey. You will anticipate and avoid the hazards (Part 3) that could pose setbacks and delays to your flight.

Long-Term Goals can be challenging to set. Even finding the time dedicated to setting them can be difficult. But they serve a great purpose within your flight plan. If a goal does not allow you to elevate, do not include it.

SHORT-TERM GOALS

Long term goals take time to accomplish. They do not happen overnight. But they happen faster when you learn how to break them into short-term goals. Looking at your goals on a quarterly basis, then focusing intently on the next 90 days, you and your team will elevate to new flight levels.

As we position our aircraft on the runway and push the throttle forward, short-term goals help create momentum. The feeling of accomplishing short-term goals may be short-lived, but they provide a long-lasting effect. They are the necessary flight levels to achieving greater success.

The Purpose of Short-Term Goals (Initial Flight Levels):

- Provide Action
- Provide Energy
- Provide Recognition

Provide Action

Short-term goals help to keep people focused on the steps necessary for forward momentum. The actions associated with each goal should be purposeful and encourage everyone to stay on track. Goal-related actions provide you and your crew with the opportunity to improve their performance and lead to better accountability.

Provide Energy

Elevating to high flight levels can seem daunting, especially because most of your crew will already feel like their plates are full. So adding more work, even on important goals, can be challenging. Short-term goals act as a boost of much-needed energy to you and your crew as they strive toward new benchmarks and targets.

Provide Recognition

Completing your plans, you accomplish dozens of short-term goals. But the greatest feeling of accomplishment will not come from reaching the goals; it will come from rewarding your team. Recognition, based on the expected results, makes the goal-setting process fun and rewarding.

SETTING YOUR FLIGHT LEVELS

5 Year Flight Levels

While it may seem unrealistic to set specific goals for five years out, this process forces you to think outside of the "plane". With your team, allow the exciting dreaming process to fuel your thoughts. Most business pilots had a long-term vision in mind when they started their businesses, but they conformed their dreams instead of transforming their thinking.

5 year goals should not be impossible, but they should be uncomfortable. That's right; get out of your comfort zone and dream-sell with your team. Let them imagine the new locations, new markets, new clients, new services, and new positions that will make up your company in 5 years.

* Identify what your company should look like in 5 years.

3 Year Flight Levels

Because most business leaders struggle to see more than five years out, your three year goals tend to be more realistic; more tangible. Five year goals may be a bit fuzzy, and understandably so. But your three year goals will unify your team by bringing your *Big Picture* into clear focus.

These important goals will allow you and your crew to become clear about specifics: revenue, margins, team size, target clients, market share, etc. Three year goals are vitally important because they establish additional buy-in from your team and increase staff retention. You are looking for people who are willing to follow you for at least the next three years.

Your three year goals may adjust over time, but they will serve as the foundation of your 1 year goals.

* Identify the goals necessary to accomplish over the next three years, to position you and your crew to hit or exceed your 5-year goals.

1 Year Flight Levels

This is where the rubber meets the road, literally. Your 1 year goals are the driving force for your business aircraft. Looking into the next year, you and your team need to focus on the goals that can be accomplished in the next 365 days. This is when the engines of your aircraft start to rev up.

This is an exciting process of planning your actions over the next year. This exercise is not about volume: the amount of goals you can list. But rather velocity: the important goals that create momentum. 1 year goals can more clearly be seen, and understood by your entire crew. I recommend setting about a dozen goals for the next year, which will be divided up into each quarter.

* Identify 12 important goals for growth over the next year.

Quarterly Flight Levels

Taking each of your twelve goals for the next year, strategically place them into each upcoming quarter. This will allow your team to focus on accomplishing three key goals per quarter. These quarterly flight levels are necessary for sustained elevation and will quickly allow your team to experience a systematic formula for accomplishing all goals: *The GOAL Formula.*

Each quarterly goal should serve as a domino, triggering the accomplishment of the next goal. The proper sequence for your business goals will help to prioritize your actions and position the team for greater success.

* Invest time with your key leaders to strategically and tactically place each goal into the appropriate quarter.

90 Day Flight

There is a huge difference between setting goals and accomplishing them. Setting goals creates excitement. Accomplishing them builds confidence. Imagine the excitement and energy created as your team strives for new goals, accomplishing them, then exceeding them.

Human beings have the innate ability to stay highly focused for about 90 days. The Marine Corps has used this psychological phenomenon for over

240 years to transform civilians into Marines. Each 90 day boot camp is filled with specific goals, objectives and actions. The title of U.S. Marine is always earned... never given.

Directly from the pages of my first book, *The GOAL Formula*, I share with business leaders the importance of optimizing and connecting the next 90 days. The next 90 days are coming and there is nothing we can do to stop them. But we can do something with them; something GREAT!

Your 90-Day Flight puts you and your team on track for your first flight level - the three goals for the next 90 days. Now, you will be able to plug them into the formula for success.

The GOAL Formula

Steps + Time + People = Accomplished Goals

Take the right steps (actions), during a specified block of time (90 days), and enlist the support of the right people (your crew) to accomplish any goal. Below are the required steps to take during your 90 Day Flight.

The 5 GREAT Steps to Accomplishing Goals:

G	Goals	–	Identify important **G**oals
R	Reasons	–	Establish powerful **R**easons
E	Expectations	–	Set high **E**xpectations
A	Actions	–	Take all of the **A**ctions necessary
T	Tracking	–	Intensely **T**rack your result

Long-term and short-term goals are paramount to the success of any organization. They allow you and your crew to aim for the skies, passing through important flight levels as you head to your destination. They help teams to become laser-focused, while increasing productivity and gaining high levels of accountability.

ELEVATE

90-Day FLIGHT PLAN

5 Year Goals:

- _____
- _____
- _____

- _____
- _____
- _____

3 Year Goals:

- _____
- _____
- _____

- _____
- _____
- _____

1 Year Goals:

- _____
- _____
- _____
- _____
- _____
- _____

- _____
- _____
- _____
- _____
- _____
- _____

E L E V A T E

90-Day FLIGHT PLAN

Q ___ Goals:

- _____
- _____
- _____

Q ___ Goals:

- _____
- _____
- _____

Q ___ Goals:

- _____
- _____
- _____

Q ___ Goals:

- _____
- _____
- _____

90 Day Goals:

- *Goal 1:* _____
- *Purpose:* _____

- *Goal 2:* _____
- *Purpose:* _____

- *Goal 3:* _____
- *Purpose:* _____

Chapter 2

Your Route

Getting and Staying on Course.

Imagine that you are a passenger on a flight. You have stowed your carry on luggage, fastened your seatbelt, and you sit back, attempting to relax as the plane begins to roll forward. Suddenly, the cockpit door opens and the pilot rushes to the back of the aircraft to check the cargo. Moments later, as the airplane speeds down the runway, the cockpit door swings open again as the pilot rushes to answer a passenger's question.

Flying above the clouds, you look out of the window to enjoy the view. But you hear footsteps as the pilot, once again, runs out of the cockpit and over to the flight attendants' station, ironing out some details about the in-flight movie. When pilots continually take their hands off the controls, and their eyes off of the flight path, how secure do you feel about arriving at your destination?

Did the pilot in the above scenario have full control of the aircraft? Most certainly not. Can a pilot guarantee to stay on course with these actions? No. Do most business pilots have control of their business aircrafts? Unfortunately, they do not, and they cannot guarantee they will stay on course.

It is detrimental to the safety of all aboard, and to the success of the flight, that pilots remain in their seats, guiding their aircraft to their locations. But everyday, business pilots leave their cockpit, attempting to handle other tasks and objectives. Working "in" their aircraft, pilots increase the risk of getting off course and missing their destination.

For the success of any business flight, it is absolutely imperative that business pilots concentrate their efforts "on" their specified *Route*; their pathway to success. Because your destination is vitally important, you must focus as much of your time as possible to getting and staying on course.

FLIGHT PATH

Aviation pilots do not merely fly in whatever direction they feel like. They follow a flight path; a route designed to ensure a successful and timely arrival at their destination. Equally important, they utilize guidance systems to stay on course, allowing the necessary tracking of their movements.

When pilots map out their routes, they utilize *airways*, legally defined paths that connect one specified location, with another. The United States Postal Service designed the first set of airways, to guide airmail pilots on their delivery routes.

These early airways allowed pilots to get on the correct path, and more importantly, to stay on that route as they traveled between major cities. Later, to guide nighttime flights, this system was enhanced, using a series of flashing lights and beacons. Now, pilots could easily follow a specific visual sequence that guided them safely to the next city. This basic principle turned the impossible to possible and still applies today for Aviators.

Most businesses, however, are operated in more of a reactionary mode, with very little thought put into the path and guidance necessary for success. Have you ever felt as though you lack the control needed to run and grow your business? If so, you are not alone.

Having a specified route is critical because it allows you to get on course, and stay on course. To do this, business pilots must keep their hands on two essential flight controls.

The 2 Essential Flight Controls for Your Route:

- **Systems**   - Get on Course
- **Accountability** - Stay on Course

By combining these two components, business pilots, and their crews, work together to maximize the effectiveness and efficiency of their flights. Proper systems, and the necessary accountability, keep pilots focused on elevating, while their crew members support every aspect of the journey.

When I begin working with business owners and leaders, I quickly detect that the majority of their frustrations stem from their inability to stay in their pilot's seat. Their cockpit functions more like a revolving door, as they consistently step away to handle recurring issues.

To complicate things, their crew fails to provide them with vital information, in the form of status reports. Without this data, the necessary adjustments, course-corrections, and improvements required to achieve greater results cannot be made. Many business pilots fail to implement accountability for fear of being perceived as a micro-manager.

But perhaps one of my most disheartening observations is when the crew becomes accustomed, or dependant, on their pilots leaving the cockpit to fill in the gaps in their systems. Leaders must strive to develop and train their teams to successfully operate the systems, accurately provide the accountability, and unquestionably take the initiative required to elevate.

Pilot's Log:
Slow down to speed up. Designing your *Route*, allows you to continually enhance your systems and accountability.

BUSINESS FLIGHT SYSTEMS - AIRWAYS TO YOUR DESTINATION

Even in an entry-level position, I quickly assessed one of the prominent weaknesses of the media company during my first three weeks on the job. Like most businesses, there were multiple examples of things that went right; flawlessly completed work. High numbers of orders were placed and completed correctly, from start to finish. Team members were happy and customers were satisfied. What more could we want?

We wanted it to happen more often. When things failed to happen flawlessly, it was like throwing a rock at a hornets nest. A mad scramble ensued as chaos reigned supreme. Some orders could not be located, while other orders had the wrong contents. Paperwork was missing and team members were confused and frustrated. Finger-pointing was our only response to the customer complaints that painfully "stung" us as we continued to repeat this head-scratching ritual.

How is it possible for things to happen perfectly one moment then disastrously wrong the next, with the same team? A mediocre system is the answer. If a system is not in place, well that is below mediocre. Our initial team was reactionary. Instead of harnessing the power generated from creating the "sense of urgency" required to run a system, we were often left drained by the energy it took to survive a "panic attack."

Focused on accomplishing the goal of doubling sales, it was crystal clear to me that we needed systems and we needed them yesterday. Fortunately, my experience in the Marine Corps taught me the importance of processes and systems. Every Marine is issued the Marine Corps Handbook, which clearly details the "how-tos" on hundreds of essential subjects.

In the two hundred page manual, everything from preparing our combat gear for inspection to accurately throwing grenades was detailed. The steps involved in making up our bunks to placing rank insignia on our uniforms were laid out in front of us, complete with vivid illustrations.

While this handbook book was filled with everything a Marine needed to know about operating as a Marine, my Air Traffic Controller duties had their own separate set of processes and systems. With mission accomplishment as a priority, and lives on the line, the commitment to excellence, in every task and objective, was not overlooked in the Marine Corps. Nor should it be overlooked in your business.

Pilot's Log:
Create high levels of excellence in your company and raise the expectations on getting things done right the first time.

Each business I coach has the ability to provide me with examples of things being done 100% correctly: sales proposals, work orders, product shipments, and time-off forms submitted. But unfortunately, instead of duplicating their successes, most companies tolerate repetitive failures.

Of course, their greatest mistake is failing to systematize their workflow; not clearing their airways for sustained business flight.

Business pilots who temporarily fix things, find themselves being involved in virtually every aspect of their company: sales, operations, accounting, HR, and marketing. They get caught up in their production lines, take customer complaint calls, try to resolve issues with vendors, and do everything in between. Everything that is, except fly their aircraft. Understanding processes and systems is the first step in adhering to your Route.

PROCESS VS. SYSTEM

"This is how we've always done it", and "This is just how I do it", are two of the most common answers I receive when I ask my clients, and their team members, about tasks that were not completed correctly. It is sadly assumed that things will go wrong in their businesses. Imagine if air traffic controllers felt that way. "Planes just crash", is not an acceptable answer.

It quickly becomes apparent that most crew members, and many business pilots, do not fully understand the difference between their processes and their systems, and it shows in their results. Below is the difference between a process and a system, with an example of a sales process and a sales system, to compare.

Process - An established series of necessary steps that ensure the completion of specific **tasks**. The way work is completed.

Sales Process (Task): Complete high levels of meaningful calls to your prospect list.

System- A unification of connected processes that ensure the completion of specific **outcomes**. The way goals are completed.

Sales System (Outcome): Develop new business, from existing and new clients by connecting the processes of prospecting, contacting, making a presentation on an appointment, setting up a new account, and following-up.

Processes and systems are critical for mission accomplishment. We re-fined both at the media company, ensuring that all work was completed correctly, every time. Systematizing workflow helped us to avoid the impact of errors. The domino effect of inadequate systems not only causes business pilots to leave the cockpit for damage-control, but it ultimately produces undesired results, leading to higher levels of disengagement from your team and frustrations for your customers. The end result is, once again, your flight is off-course.

FLIGHT SYSTEMS

Systems take the guess work out of the important tasks necessary to run your business and the priority objectives required to grow it. Many organizations feel the impact of wasted time and money, as their people guess and hope for success. The same time, however, can be invested in running detailed systems, allowing teams to experience predictable results.

If you have the desire to *ELEVATE*, you need specific systems, run by skilled team members, and monitored by leaders who are focused on excellence. But what systems are most important? The most important systems are the ones required for elevation; the systems that lift your teams' performance and their results to new levels.

While every business is unique, and may possess multiple processes and protocols, you and your team should narrow them down to a handful of relevant systems. This is how you can simplify, streamline, and unify your entire team to elevate your business aircraft.

Key Flight Systems:

Business Elevation System - Your path for strategic planning, setting tactical actions, and accomplishing short-term and long-term business goals.

Leadership Connection System - Your path for identifying and developing leaders at all levels, who continually empower team members to support the elevation of your business.

3-D Sales System - Your path for sales excellence by increasing business from new and existing customers, through contacting and marketing.

Operations System - Your path for processing and delivering your products and services at the highest levels of excellence.

Team Training System - Your path for recruiting, on-boarding, and providing continual training and incentives to all team members.

As a small, but rapidly elevating media business, other processes also supported our five key systems. Our marketing process allowed us to reach target clients and prospects with our unique, dynamic message. But this process was used within our sales system. Our HR processes, such as hiring and firing, on-boarding and promoting, were incorporated into our Leadership Development System and Team Training System.

Investing the time necessary to develop our Key Flight Systems, also allowed us to eliminate redundant processes as we trained our entire team on how to follow them properly. We soon discovered that all of our Key Flight Systems worked together, making each one more effective, which allowed us to unify our efforts and stay on course.

You and your leaders must not only identify, but define the systems that will keep you in the pilot's seat and your flight on track.

DEFINING YOUR SYSTEMS

Once you have identified the Key Flight Systems that will support your route, you must define each system, taking every step (process) and simplifying them. This allows your crew to get on the same page and head in the same direction. Each system will have its own unique workflow; a workflow that will be constantly enhanced as you *ELEVATE*.

In the media industry, our services were highly technical, often including pages of broadcast specifications from our clients for each job we processed. Our Operations System needed to account for this high level of detail as each order flowed through our system. To reaffirm our commitment to our flight, we hung a framed sign in each department that read:

"Complete Every Order Correctly and Deliver it On Time."

The details of any particular order ranged from 12-channel audio configuration for high definition video elements to frame-by-frame digital restoration of feature films. We converted programs from American video standards to the standards of other countries, while editing hundreds of hours of footage, and creating file-based media formats.

We systematized our workflow to duplicate our successes and eliminate our failures. We transformed our complex work into our simple Operations System. These seven steps allowed our team to complete each order correctly and deliver them on-time. We had achieved success on many past orders, so we planned to make it a habit on all future orders.

Our core leaders, including myself, followed many orders through our system, as we designed the optimum steps for success. Team members were constantly asked for their insights on improvements. When our crew made a suggestion, especially one that was implemented, they felt valued and they were more committed to higher levels of initiative. Engage your team by including them in the process of finding solutions.

Before creating our system, we sold roughly $150,000 of media services per month, with nearly 15% of our orders having errors. These unnecessary mistakes caused us to re-do orders or refund our customers. Neither choice allowed elevation. Both kept us in an endless "holding pattern."

By locking down the steps in our systems, our diligence paid off many times over. With the proper implementation and training, our systems allowed us to soar to over $600,000 in monthly sales, while reducing our errors from 15% to .35%. Time invested up front, paid off on the back end.

On the next page, is the exact seven-step system we used to successfully complete over 1,200 uniquely complex orders each month. Our systems kept us on route as we elevated to over 300% sales growth, and arrived at our first destination; our second facility in Burbank, California.

7-STEP OPERATIONS SYSTEM

STEP 1 – ORDER VERIFICATION
- Sales Specialist uses Fact Finder to gather important information.
- Sales Specialist completes required fields and submits Order Form.
- Operations Specialist reviews Order Form – returns if incomplete.

STEP 2 – DATA ENTRY
- Scheduler helps client place order.
- Scheduler enters all order information into software.
- Supervisor completes Checkpoint - transitions order to next Dept.

STEP 3 – PURCHASE ORDERS
- Supervisor completes Checkpoint – assigns order for processing.
- Operator/Editor processes the order according to the Work Order.
- Supervisor completes Checkpoint – transitions order to Labeling.

STEP 4 – LABELING
- Supervisor completes Checkpoint – assigns order for QC/Labeling.
- Labeler performs QC Spot Check, as required then labels all media.
- Supervisor completes Checkpoint – transitions order to Operations.

STEP 5 – SHIPPING
- Scheduler verifies the order is complete and pricing is correct.
- Supervisor completes Checkpoint – transitions order to Delivery.

STEP 6 – INVOICING
- Scheduler notifies client that the order is complete.
- Scheduler reviews the entire order prior to delivery.

STEP 7 – FINALIZING
- Scheduler records payment and files the order for Accounting.
- Supervisor reviews all filed orders and forwards to Accounting.
- Team Member follows up with client – prepares for next order.

Our systems were a key factor for our success. They promoted teamwork and broke down the imaginary walls that existed between departments. In our Operations System alone, the following departments were included: Sales, Accounting, Media Processing, Editorial, Labeling, and of course, Operations.

Our seven step system involved the efforts our Sales Team, Operations Supervisors, Schedulers, Machine Room Supervisors, Tape Operators, Editors, Labeling Supervisors, and Labelers. Our entire crew was involved in these important steps, which impacted our ability to remain on our route.

Pilot's Log:
Leaders use systems, not just to produce better work, but to develop better teams.

Because our sales goals were the driving factors for elevating, I focused heavily on making sure that our sales efforts were predictable and profitable. We narrowed our Sales System down to five important steps; the five gears needed to consistently turn and provide power to our sales engine.

We wanted to ensure the highest probability of success for our sales team, and every crew member who supported their efforts. Again, it made sense to complete every sales task, "Correct and On-Time." Each step in our Sales System was detailed in our Sales Manual, which provided strategies and techniques for continued success.

The 5 Sales Gears:

1. **Prospecting** - The art of deciding whom to contact

2. **Contacting** - The mastery of setting the next appointment

3. **Presenting** - Moving from content to connection

4. **Set-Up** - Preparing the order or the account for success

5. **Follow-Up** - The true testament of our commitment level

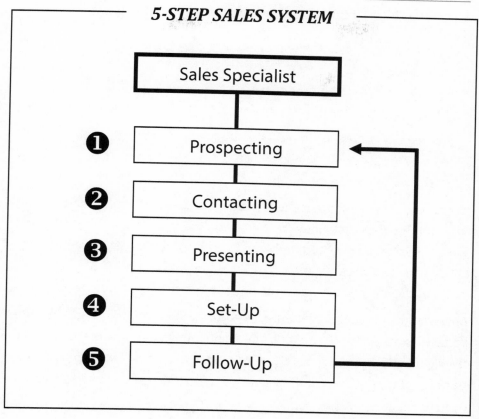

The time invested in designing our systems did not slow us up. The orders and tasks we focused on were the same orders and tasks that would have caused us to leave the cockpit when something went wrong. Our systems kept us in control of our flight and focused on our route.

When I began working at the media company, our employees said, "Here's how we've always done it." But our careful attention to detail, not only communicated the importance of each step within our systems, it transformed their dialogue. As we stayed on course and began to *ELEVATE*, it was common to hear, "Here's how we get it done right," from our crew.

Well-defined systems allow businesses to scale as they strategically connect with the necessary accountability to stay on track.

More detailed sales strategies can be found in my book, *3-D Sales*.

ACCOUNTABILITY - YOUR GUIDANCE SYSTEMS

Whether we fly to an amazing vacation spot, or we excitedly await the arrival of a beloved family member arriving home for the holidays, we all step into the airport and do the exact same thing. We walk to the nearest monitor and check the arrival and departure information of the flights.

While there is countless amounts of data that could be posted, it is kept simple and to the point. Typically listed: the departure city, airline, flight number, arrival time, gate number, and most importantly, the status.

As we anxiously look up at the screen, we hope to see two magic words, "On-Time." But occasionally, we see the dreaded word, "Delayed." What thoughts go through your mind when you see that word? There is almost nothing more frustrating, than a delayed flight. You may spend additional hours in the airport, or worse yet, be required to come back the next day.

Airports are phenomenally diligent at accountability; providing us with updated status reports. Having the right information allows us to take the right actions. Unfortunately, most businesses do not excel in this area. Business flights are indefinitely delayed, with few people even aware.

With the creation of your Flight Systems, the next step to staying on your route, and arriving "On Time," is to develop the guidance systems that will allow you and your crew to track the movements of your aircraft, make the necessary adjustments, and elevate to new levels. Where performance is measured performance increases.

You cannot merely implement systems without the accountability to track all of the important information needed to make better decisions. Avoid delays in your business and ensure that every flight departs and arrives on time by increasing the accountability with your crew.

PROPER ACCOUNTABILITY ELIMINATES MICROMANAGEMENT

As an air traffic controller, I monitored only the essential pieces of information needed to support the pilots flying the aircraft. I was never accused of micro-management because the data was essential to the flight. Just as your business has various departments, and important information, the air traffic control system utilizes key data, from different departments, to keep the pilots in their seats and in control of their flights.

Ground Control - Utilizes information to allow pilots to guide their aircraft, to and from the airfield to the runway.

Flight Data - Uses information such as weather changes, airport ground delays, and runway closures to provide take off and landing clearance.

Local Control - Utilizes information to guide pilots who are in the air, within the five-mile ATA (Air Traffic Area), surrounding the control tower.

Radar Control - Uses information to *"Track the Blip,"* on their radar monitors, as aircraft travel hundreds of miles in their airspace.

Again, there is an infinite amount of data that air traffic controllers can track, but they only utilize the key information required to ensure that flights stay on course, and arrive at their destinations.

TRACK THE BLIP

Business accountability, sometimes referred to by frustrated employees as micro-management, often comes in two sizes: next-to nothing, and way-too-much. Sitting with my new clients, I enjoy asking to see the reports they use to "Track the Blip," to monitor the status of their flight. I either receive nothing, or I am handed piles of confusing paperwork.

Whether a business pilot operates with no report, or too many reports, the end result usually is the same. They are unable to assess the status of their flight. The crew operates the business with their heads in the clouds, while their planes remain on the ground.

Pilots, who lack critical data, find themselves leaving the cockpit, endlessly searching for the information necessary for success, and team members find themselves lacking a clear understanding of where they are going.

With systems, you and your crew can *Track the Blip* together. You will identify the key information required for staying on course, while simultaneously enhancing the dialogue in your organization. Your crew will begin to have purpose with all forms of their communication and correspondence.

STATE OF MOTION

In aviation, guidance systems allow for the calculation of the changes in position, velocity, altitude, and other aspects required to remain on a specific trajectory. Staying on course is largely based on the information regarding the aircraft's state of motion.

Even the slightest deviation, perhaps one degree off course, can have a dramatic impact on the pilot's ability to arrive at a destination thousands of miles away. Accountability in your business accomplishes two purposes, with regard to your company's state of motion.

2 Key Purposes of Accountability:

1. Change the perceptions of "micro-management" to "tracking"
2. Create reports with the essential data required for course-correction

So, the big question is, "What do I track?" Quite simply, you track the status of your systems. You pay particular attention to your **Business Elevation System**, **Leadership Development System**, **Sales System**, **Operations System**, and **Team Training System**; the systems required for elevation.

Technology is both a blessing and a curse to today's business pilots, providing detailed reports, summaries, and statistics on every conceivable aspect of their business. To ELEVATE, it is imperative to track progress as you strive to reach your flight levels. You are either on track or you are not.

You monitor progress to remain on course. If you are not heading in the right direction, you and your crew immediately make the necessary course-corrections to get back en route.

One of the first areas to track is the performance and results in your sales system. You can monitor everything from phones dials and e-mails, to conversations and appointments. You can analyze proposals, bids, and quotes, and assess orders placed, new clients developed, referrals earned, and profit margins. But ultimately you need to track the information that increases your ability to grow; to *ELEVATE* successfully.

STATUS REPORTS

In aviation, the status of each flight is the primary focus for everyone involved. Both the crew in the air and the support staff on the ground pay particular attention to vital information. Status can be tracked by using simple flight progress strips in the air traffic control tower to using real-time GPS technologies.

To *ELEVATE* you must track your sales efforts and results, track orders through operations, track the growth of your leaders, and the training of your team members. Instead of being bogged down with a mountain of data, use *Status Reports* to give your team a snapshot of where you are, in relation to where you are going.

In our sales department, we used a Daily Sales Report to monitor our performance. We looked at the status of each individual sales specialist and the status of our sales efforts as a company. Based on a high volume of orders (1,200+ per month), this daily snapshot allowed us to take action immediately. Based on your volume, you may prefer a weekly snapshot, or another frequency that works best with your company.

In addition to our sales "actuals" we took a close look at the actions that were occuring to drive our sales results. Each day, we reviewed a report of our team's performance. We reviewed their calls, proposals, appointments, orders, and volume. If their calls were high, but their appointments were low, we could help them to adjust their strategies.

Similarly, if they had low numbers of orders, but a high volume of proposals, we could take a closer look at each proposal, providing them with ideas on how to increase the successful conversion to orders. We only tracked what we were prepared to course-correct. But everything we tracked was deemed as priority objectives.

Yes, we achieved high levels of elevation and we arrived at our amazing destinations. When I'm asked how we did it, I would have to say that each day we course-corrected our way to success, which was only possible by tracking the performance of our systems.

Working with new clients, one of the first Status Reports I create is a sales tracking report, often called a Sales Report, Sales Snapshot, or Sales Scorecard. You can give it a name that helps to enhance your team identity. But understand that it will only work if it tracks the correct information

Below is an example of the basic status report I use in many organizations to *Track the Blip* on their sale efforts. In this example, we set out to identify the top five performers in each category. But one of the first results of having a Status Report for these actions was an increase in performance from all twenty of their sales representatives.

Daily Sales Scorecard

Calls		Proposals		Orders		Volume	
Maggie	53	Glen	13	Glen	08	Rick	$ 8,768
Glen	45	Carol	11	Darrly	06	Maggie	$ 6,756
Rick	39	Darryl	08	Rick	05	Darryl	$ 5,945
Darryl	37	Maggie	05	Maggie	03	Glen	$ 5,693
Carol	25	Rick	03	Carol	01	Carol	$ 4,982

Was this report welcomed with open arms by each member of the sales team when it was rolled out? Of course not. It was a change, and for many, an uncomfortable one at first. To some, it was a micro-management tool. However, by being consistent, and staying the course with this report, the leaders in the sales team were able to identify areas of much-needed support, guidance, and course-correction.

During our first Sales Meeting, when asked about their projections for the upcoming week, almost the entire team responded with, "I don't know." The year after implementing this report, 90% of their sales team ended the year with greater sales results, and profit margins, than the year before. Also, their understanding of their own performance increased.

Now, each sales meeting is filled with detailed projections for the upcoming week, and the team provides the business pilot (the owner) with the monthly and quarterly forecasting she needs to guide her aircraft and stay on course.

My experience as the vice president taught me that our sales accountability was critical for mission accomplishment. In fact, leaders from each department were present in our Sales Meetings to get a clearer understanding of our sales status. They returned to their teams, with this information, so they could make the necessary adjustments to keep us on course.

In our Operations Department, our Status Report was called a "Due Report." It told us when orders were due. It doesn't get any more simple than that. But on some days we had over 100 orders due, up to 75-80 new orders arriving, and dozens of other orders currently being processed with later due dates.

We had a lot of plates spinning, with shifts extending 24 hours per day to complete all of the work. This one report allowed us a quick, but accurate snapshot of our order status. The Due Report was so critical to our success, that our Operations Supervisor updated this report "Every hour on the hour" during normal business hours. It was intensely monitored by our other supervisors and their team members.

As a team, we *Tracked the Blip* for each order, with exact precision. Listing only the client name, project title, type of work, due date and due time, and these five pieces of critical data allowed us to involve multiple crew members in the success of our system. Remember, it also allowed us to move the dial on our internal errors to under 1%.

Pilot's Log:

Focus the efforts of your entire team to getting on course and staying on course, to avoid delays.

Chapter 3

Your ETA

It's About Time!

With the loud bang of metal trash cans being tossed down the squad bay, the recruits of Platoon 1095 received another morning wake-up call from our drill instructors. It was 0430 (4:30 am) and within minutes of the DI's "alarm clock" going off, we were dressed, our bunks were properly made, and we were marching to the chow hall. Yet another well-planned day of our 90-day journey was about to begin.

Basic training presented one clear destination at the end of our route: the parade deck. Nearly every day our drill instructors marched us to the very spot we would be graduating, provided we could stay on course. Each Friday, graduation ceremonies were in progress and recruits received their final order from their senior drill instructors. With a last about-face movement, each recruit became a Marine.

Our destination was of the highest importance to me and to each of my fellow recruits. Although our route was challenging, we had our ETA: November 13, 1987. How important was that date to me? It was so important to graduate, and leave boot camp as a United States Marine, that I wrote that date on every page of my handbook. I saw it each day. and I sent letters home, to family and friends, announcing this date.

Platoon 1095 moved with a sense of urgency, with every task and objective we were faced with. Earning the title of U.S. Marine did not happen overnight. It took time and not a single minute of our 90 days was wasted. By having an ETA, a timeline that motivated and inspired me, I accomplished one of the most important goals of my entire life. I graduated from boot camp on November 13, 1987 and joined an elite brotherhood that I have been a part of since the day I stepped off of the bus.

One of the greatest common denominators linking all successful business-es is that it takes time to achieve greater results. It takes time to develop your plan, build your team, and position your business for success. Reach-ing your destination does not happen overnight and many business lead-ers fail to commit to the time required for elevation.

It is typically agreed that consistent success is a long path of diligent work. Yet most business pilots dream that they are the exception to that rule; that their planes will fly on auto-pilot to their destinations. Hope is not an option when it comes to elevating your results. While we achieved high levels of elevation and success at the media company, it took nearly five years to arrive at our second location.

Like many businesses, we experienced challenges, difficulties, and other hazards as we elevated. The recession of 2008 was a major obstacle. But by constantly focusing on our flight plan, we were able to set and adjust our timeframes for success. I will be bold enough to say that without im-portant timelines, we may have followed the path that many of our com-petitors did. They closed the doors to their aircraft, permanently.

If your destination is important, and you are committed to following your route, then setting your ETA is a critically important step. When your flight encounters any obstacles, you must immediately adjust the actions and timelines to compensate for the course-corrections. Just as a delayed, or re-routed flight will maneuver and adjust the times to arrive at the des-tination, your crew must learn to do the same.

Pilot's Log:
Most people do not find the time to succeed. Business pilots make the time.

Marketing guru Seth Godin once mentioned that "It takes about six years of hard work to become an overnight success." The business pilots of to-day's most successful, household-name companies understand the im-portance of time, and they remained committed to their success, despite their challenges and set-backs.

Amazon.com - Founded in 1994 by Jeff Bezos. The company was taken public three years later, making him a multi-billionaire. A rare case that still took a few years.

- "Overnight Success" in 3 years

Yahoo! - Founded in 1994 by Jerry Yang and David Filo. In 1996, the company was taken public, but still required about three more years for true financial success.

- "Overnight Success" in 5 years

Facebook - Founded as "Facemash" in 2003 by Mark Zuckerberg. In 2005, Facebook was showing a yearly net loss of $3.63 million. Five years later, it achieved nearly 400 million users worldwide.

- "Overnight Success" in 7 years

Google - Founded in 1996 by Larry Page and Sergey Brin. By 1999, few people had heard of the company. Five years later, the company was taken public with a market capitalization of $23B.

- "Overnight Success" in 8 years

Microsoft - Founded in 1975 by Bill Gates. It took six years to develop a contract with IBM to provide their PC base operating system. It took another five years before Microsoft went public in 1986.

- "Overnight Success" in 11 years

Apple - Founded in 1976 by Steve Jobs. It took eight years to get on the map with the launch of Macintosh in 1984. Struggling through the 80s and 90s, it wasn't until iMac was launched in 1998 that Jobs considered it a success.

- "Overnight Success" in 22 years

Keep in mind that these companies are typically recognized as some of the fastest growing organizations in the past few decades. But their potential to *ELEVATE* is no different than your potential to *ELEVATE*. These business pilots consistently put in the time necessary, matched with hard work, to reach amazing flight levels. Are you committed to the time required for your success?

I encourage my clients to be *patiently persistent*. Most want to be an overnight success, arriving immediately at their destinations. But learning how to set your ETAs and make the necessary course-corrections is a discipline that will serve you and your crew well. Virtually every successful business required substantial amounts of time to achieve elevation.

TODAY IS THE DAY

You cannot accomplish anything yesterday. It is over; gone forever. There is no business leader in history that can recapture lost or wasted time. But you can start to avoid the time traps of failure by focusing on important timelines and the mindset required for success.

As a business pilot, time is a precious commodity; more valuable than money. You cannot afford to waste it, or worse yet, pay your team to waste it. As business owners, we understand that we can lose money and get it back. We can lose people and hire new ones. Some have even lost their entire business and started over. But time is different. You will never get it back. You must protect it like a mother bear protects her cubs.

There are 1,825 days involved in your 5-year flight levels, 1,095 days in your 3-year flight levels, and well, you know that there are 365 days in your 1-year flight levels. Each day is critically important. What if you could master your time? What if you could help your team members to take control of their time? Could you accomplish your goals on time? Yes.

As you learn Time Mastery, you can also begin to collapse the time frames associated with your goals and position your team to achieve greater results sooner than planned. What if you could elevate to new flight levels ahead of schedule? Imagine how GREAT that would feel.

When I launched Think GREAT in 2008, I knew that writing my first book was going to be an important goal for the growth of my company and a major factor in my ability to impact people with my goal-setting concepts.

Like most goals, the idea of writing a book was intimidating. I had never done it before and the steps involved seemed daunting. How long would it take me? Would I need to invest two years, three years, or more?

A close friend had told me that he heard, "If you write a page per day, you can have a book completed in a year." That was music to my ears and I felt the hope flowing through me. I now had a possible timeline. But as the vice president of a fast-growing media company, not only did I want to control my time even more, I wanted to collapse those timeframes.

My destination was so important that I adjusted my route and set the goal of writing my book in six months. Instead of one page per day, I committed to two pages per day. 2009 was now here and I set the goal of completing my book. By launching two, back-to-back 90 Day Flight plans, I set my ETA and was holding a copy of my first book by September 1, 2009.

Because I learned to set ETAs and I focused on mastering my time, *ELEVATE* is now the sixth book in my collection. Number seven, coming soon.

Pilot's Log:

Become a master of time and control more than your schedule; control your destiny.

RELATIONSHIP TO TIME

When I begin working with my clients, I quickly assess how they utilize their time. Most business pilots are busy, night and day; busy from start to finish. But are they productive? There is a huge difference between the two; the difference between going in circles on the airfiled (busy) and reaching your dreams in the sky (productive). They move at a fast pace, but they fail to produce the results needed to *ELEVATE*.

Corporate Culture is one of the biggest buzz-phrases of recent times, and business leaders strive to create an environment that allows them to grow their employees into strong, goal-accomplishing team members. Unfortunately, too many end up settling for a culture designed to make their staff happy, rather than challenging them to accomplish more with their time. As leaders they strive to be liked, rather than be respected.

Let me speak frankly, as a leadership coach. If you want to elevate, it is paramount that you create a unifying culture that promotes leadership, teamwork, goal-setting, and high levels of results. Foster an environment where your team embraces the challenges set by their leaders. Develop the crew that will be "happy" working in a culture that encourages their growth and inspires them to set and achieve their ETAs.

Pilot's Log:
Your culture is based on the level of your tolerance for poor performance.

SETTING YOUR ETA

When a plane departs, it is merely one of many flights scheduled for that aircraft. Most commercial airlines fly each plane in their fleet at least six days per week, making multiple stops every day. Arrival times are critically important as they significantly impact the next flight. Setting and adjusting ETAs is a vital step to remaining on route to your destination.

By establishing ETAs for our goals, we created a sense of urgency that spread throughout the media company. In 2004, we launched our one year goal of increasing sales revenue by at least 15%. With our timeline in place, and our team focused on our goals, we concentrated on the ETAs within our 90-Day Flight Plan; the time we could control.

We ended far better than we had projected that year, achieving 23.99% sales growth. Understanding the importance of time, we stayed on route and collapsed time frames on many of our quarterly objectives. The next year, we set the goal of 25% sales growth. The ETAs set in our back-to-back 90-Day Flight Plans, allowed us to grow sales by over 50% that year.

These results did not happen in a lackluster culture. Nor did they happen with a crew of "busy" people running around wasting time. By focusing on our systems, we saved valuable time, which was reinvested into our goals. By tracking our performance and course-correcting our efforts, we saved additional time, which was invested back into our goals. Our team moved with a purpose because we established ETAs in our 90-Day Flight Plans.

Each goal you plan to accomplish during any 90 day period will require a specific amount of objectives, which must be achieved. The objectives you identify are the stepping stones on the path to your goals. When business leaders fail to attach the necessary time lines to their goals and objectives, their aircraft are rendered immobile and their teams become ineffective.

As an executive business leader, I was heavily involved in the goal setting process; creating our plan. But I was not involved in each action required to meet every objective. After all, I was helping to fly the plane. But I properly delegated the tasks and authority necessary to accomplish much through the efforts of our crew. Like a mother bear, I protected our ETAs.

Without due dates, agreed upon by the entire crew, our flight would have lost much of its meaning; its purpose; its ability to move us. As with any business, challenges arose, but our crew was able to rise above those difficult circumstances by staying focused on our ETAs. By controlling our time, we not only handled issues with greater resolve, we elevated to new flight levels and arrived at our destination.

Pilot's Log:

Carpe Diem - Sieze the Day. What are you going to do with the time you have?

TIME MASTERY

Your relationship to time directly impacts your distance from your destination. Where will you be on day 91? Will your flight be listed as On-Time, Delayed, or Cancelled? There is no other option. While time is in limited quantity, it is unlimited in its value, especially as you learn how to do more with less. What you and your team do each day will translate into your results on the final day of your flight plan.

To elevate to high levels, the ETAs in our 90-Day Flight Plans were more than suggestions, they were purposeful commands, followed at the highest levels of dedication. A dedicated crew will not only control time, but will collapse it, shrinking the distances between each flight level. A Flight Crew that is determined to arrive on time can be an unstoppable force.

In the Marine Corps, as you may imagine, everything we did was done with a quick pace. I learned how to accomplish many things in very short blocks of time. I took three valuable ETA disciplines with me into the corporate world; the same three time disciplines you and your team can use to transform your ETAs into realities.

Three ETA Disciplines:

- Create a Sense of Urgency
- Transform Busy Work into Productive Actions
- Harness the Power of a Schedule

Create a Sense of Urgency

Seeing your crew move is exciting, but seeing them move with a purpose is what precedes elevation. A powerful destination, shared by the leaders on a regular basis, will create a sense of urgency that inspires your team to work smarter, not just harder.

Creating a sense of urgency makes *sense* and every business leader would agree with its merits. But where do you start? How do you increase velocity with your people? Quite simply, business pilots must lead by example, moving with a purpose. Pick up your own pace as you move throughout your office, your warehouse, your production line.

In addition, set ETAs with a minimum time to achieve the objective. Timelines should not be impossible, but rather challenging. A challenging ETA will create momentum among your crew. Loose timelines are rarely met, but tight timelines are seldom missed.

To further add to the sense of urgency required for elevation, announce the ETAs for each objective to other team members. Announcing each

ETA, and providing regular status updates on the progress, not only validates your accountability, but creates increased engagement in other team members. Without a sense of urgency, goals become lost in the clouds and remain unaccomplished year after year.

Pilot's Log:
Without a sense of urgency, even the greatest momentum will lose its steam.

Transform Busy to Productive

Business pilots must strive to change movement into momentum. Being on the move is different than creating the momentum needed for elevation. As a business coach, I have discovered that many employees strive to appear busy, more concerned with others seeing them moving, rather than being seen producing results.

Productive crew members, however, are vital to your ETAs. People witness much more than their movement, they experience their momentum. Productive crew members are on a mission. While busy people use movement to appear productive, productive people use momentum to achieve results.

Just look at the difference between running on a treadmill and running on a track. Yes, both serve a purpose in regards to your health, and both require movement. But only one allows your momentum to physically move you along your route. ETAs transform movement into momentum by eliminating busy work and increasing productive actions.

ETAs provide clarity, allowing business pilots and crew members to prioritize their time. Many busy people have long To Do Lists, often overwhelmed by the sheer volume of tasks they have noted. Productive people are unique, using important timelines to focus on the key objectives necessary to accomplish the three goals detailed in their 90-Day Flight Plans.

Last but not least, busy transforms to productive when *value* is added to the equation. Nobody is ever too busy to accomplish something when importance is attached. They miraculously find the time when the results mean something to them. Busy people rarely have time to add anything new to their schedules. But the same people can pull off the impossible when they plan to go on vacation, prepare for a review, or strive for a bonus.

Pilot's Log:
Busy people have movement as their mission. Productive people have a mission for their movement.

Use a Schedule

I have seen people plan vacations with the greatest attention to detail, in the hopes of maximizing every minute of a dream destination. Shouldn't your 90-Day Flight Plan deserve that same type of attention? Your destination is important and the use of a schedule will put you and your team in full control of the time required for success.

Without a schedule, business pilots often find themselves at the end of a long day, feeling unproductive. Even though they woke up ready to take on the world, or at least to position their aircraft for take off, they feel as if nothing significant was accomplished. Exhausted, yes. Elevated, no.

Without a detailed daily schedule, it's all too easy for this to happen. With a barrage of endless meetings, constant interruptions, and urgent last-minute problems, business pilots can spend countless hours on the ground, investing little to no time in the progress of their plans.

After a long march, the recruits of Platoon 1095 began a full assault on the obstacle course. With the summer heat beating down on us, we climbed, jumped, scaled our way up, and negotiated the wooden obstacles stretching into the sky. After, with sweat dripping down our faces, we stood at attention, awaiting our next command.

One of our drill instructors removed his cover (his hat), and pulled a 3x5 card out. Quickly reviewing it, he placed it back in and rested his cover perfectly atop his tightly shaved head. With a loud, "Right face," we turned in unison. "Forward... march", resonated confidently from his mouth and we marched to our next assignment. Leaving nothing to chance, every action of every day was planned and scheduled on our route.

When the destination is that important, you owe it to yourself and to your team to leave no room for error. A schedule helps to maximize every minute of every day. Imagine what the next 90 days in your organization will be like as you create a sense of urgency, transform busy work into productive actions, and adhere to a schedule designed for success.

Scheduling your day is the art of planning your activities and the discipline of sticking with them. The proper schedule will put you in control of your time and will empower your crew to duplicate your efforts. Your daily schedule will lead into the planning of each week and each month during your 90-Day Flight Plan.

A daily schedule will account for all of the actions required to achieve the monthly objectives you set, and to stay on track with each ETA. Most importantly, prepare each day in advance, preferably by mapping out your actions the night before. At the end of your day, analyze your schedule to identify areas for improvement.

Pilot's Log:
Failing to plan is planning to fail.

90-DAY FLIGHT PLAN

The wheels of your business aircraft are now on the runway. Your 90-Day Flight Plan is one of the most exciting steps in elevation. You and your crew will take the three important goals for the quarter and establish the objectives required to accomplish them. Your plan will become a living breathing document, unifying your crew and allowing them to become a team of goal-accomplishing business crew members.

How important are the next three months to your business? Well, if you fail to accomplish goals in the next 90 days, how can you expect to accomplish them over the next year, three years, or five years? The next three months are critically important, and the good news is that you and your team can control every day.

Failure is not an option. Simplicity is again a key factor for elevation, as you and your team transfer your three goals to your 90-Day Flight Plan. Let's take a closer look at the eight key components to arrive on time and support the successful accomplishment of your goals.

The Key Components of your 90-Day Flight Plan:

- Opportunity
- Goals
- Purpose
- Key Crew Members
- Monthly Objectives & ETAs
- Strategy
- Budget
- Conclusion

Opportunity - Describe, in detail, the fortunes within reach: new opportunities for organic growth, profitability, team morale, personal growth, and professional development. Share the opportunities that require your business to *ELEVATE*.

Goals - List each important goal that will allow you to attain the opportunities in front of you, describing them with clarity and certainty.

Purpose - Underneath each goal, write the specific purpose of that goal. State "why" this goal needs to be accomplished for your business.

Key Crew Members - Goals are not accomplished alone. List the crew members who will be working on the accomplishment of each goal.

Monthly Objectives & ETAs - List each month in your 90-Day Flight Plan. Under each month, create a check box for each objective (step) that needs to be taken to accomplish the goal. Assign each objective a firm ETA, the specific date the objective will be met. Also, list the key team member, the person who will be the "Crew Chief" for this objective; responsible for its success.

Strategy - In this section, detail the strategies required to accomplish each goal, such as the frequency of your meetings and accountability.

Budget - Each goal may require a specific financial investment. Ensure that this important step is completed and that you and your crew fully understand what the return on this investment will be.

Conclusion - What positive impact will your company experience when you *ELEVATE* to the flight levels necessary to capture the opportunities at hand? The impact should be empowering, engaging, and exciting. The greater the impact, the stronger the buy-in from everyone involved. Your impact should inspire and motivate your crew to form another 90-Day Flight Plan to attain more opportunities.

For the sample 90-Day Flight Plan, on pages 68 and 69, I have listed only Goal #1 and the other components associated to that goal. Each of your three goals may have a varying number of different objectives, ETAs, strategies, and budgets. It is up to you and your team to analyze each goal and determine the actions necessary to accomplish them.

Pilot's Log:
Keep your 90-Day Flight Plan, short, sweet, and to the point.

ELEVATE

90-Day FLIGHT PLAN

Impact:

By elevating to our 3 Quarterly Flight Levels, XYZ Company will be able to increase our sales reach, empower our team members, and improve customer satisfaction.

We will be on route to achieve our mission and help to create a better environment for our team.

Goal #1:

Develop and launch Phone Zone to increase outbound calls by 50% for all 10 sales reps. Total daily calls = 50 per day, per rep.

Purpose:

To increase the quality calling time of our sales team, without interruptions. To allow the time needed for building better relationships and achieving greater results.

Key Crew Members:

- Bob Davis, Sales Director
- Kelly Smith, Sales Supervisor
- Adam Turner, Operations Director

Month 1 Objectives - Goal #1

- ☐ Develop Phone Zone schedule - Crew Chief (Bob) - Jul. 14
- ☐ Review Phone Zone initiative with the sales team - Crew Chief (Kelly) - Jul. 27
- ☐ Review support requirements from sales team to ensure a solid Phone Zone - Crew Chief (Adam) - Jul. 30

ELEVATE
90-Day FLIGHT PLAN

Month 2 Objectives - Goal # 1

- [ ] Launch Phone Zone - Crew Chief (Kelly) - Aug. 01
- [ ] Collect Weekly Tracking - Crew Chief (Bob) - Aug. 07
- [ ] Review support requirements from sales team to ensure a solid Phone Zone - Crew Chief (Adam) - Aug. 21

Month 3 Objectives - Goal # 1

- [ ] Begin focused Phone Zone - 50 calls per day, per sales rep - Crew Chief (Bob) - Sep . 01
- [ ] Review Phone Progress - Crew Chief (Kelly) - Sep. 15

Strategy:

Regulary review and analyze the call volume of each sales rep. Identify any obstacles in their path to success and remove through workflow enhancements and training.

Budget:

Possibly one additional operations specialist to handle initial data entry needs and incoming inquiries. Workflow enhancements may eliminate the need for an additional team member.

Conclusion:

By increasing outbound calls by 50%, our total number of calls will elevate to 500 per day - 10,000 per month. Based on our current sales conversion ratios, the additional calls could yield between 15-20% additional sales growth for this corporate year, further enhancing the company-wide incentive plan.

Part II

Aircrew Development

The higher we soar, the smaller we appear to those who cannot fly.

~ Friedrich Nietzsche

Part II

Aircrew Development

The Human Factor.

"I, Erik Therwanger, do solemnly swear that I will support and defend the Constitution of the United States against all enemies, foreign and domestic; that I will bear true faith and allegiance to the same; and that I will obey the orders of the President of the United States and the orders of the officers appointed over me, according to regulations and the Uniform Code of Military Justice. So help me God."

Before I was allowed to begin boot camp; before I was trained to earn the title of U.S. Marine, I raised my right hand and took that oath. I was eighteen years old and this was a critical step of the on-boarding process to join the ranks of our nation's military. Our oath identified a commitment level from each member, before the significant investment of time, money, and resources were poured into our development. Yes, mission accomplishment is that important.

Most businesses do not require team members to take an oath before they begin work. But with 72% disengagement in the workplace, perhaps it wouldn't be a bad idea. You have a business to run and grow, and you need to develop your team; the Flight Crew that will support the elevation of your company. How do you put together a dream team of committed crew members?

While most business planning programs dive deep into the processes and systems needed for success, they merely touch down on the human factor required for elevation. They often fail to provide business leaders with the relevant techniques and strategies required to assemble, develop, and position the team for growth. As a U.S. Marine, I understand the unparalleled importance for teamwork.

As leaders, we accomplish things through the efforts of others; our team members. This includes every action, objective, goal, and destination identified in our Flight Plans. Fulfilling our mission and vision rests on who we allow, yes allow, to participate in our flight. Achieving elevation and taking our businesses to the next level comes down to the selection of our Flight Crew and the development of their skills.

Engagement, engagement, engagement. Strive to form your crew and position them to contribute to the success of your plan, at the highest levels possible. Engaged teams can achieve over 200% greater results than disengaged teams. At the media company, we elevated past 300%. But the secret to our success was not a secret at all. It was our crew.

Your business in not an unmanned drone, nor should it be permanently set on auto-pilot, hoping for a successful flight. The performance of your crew will either help your organization to *ELEVATE*, or it will move your aircraft around endlessly on the airfield. The choice is yours.

You no longer need to hope that your team will miraculously make the shift from disengaged and low-performing employees to engaged and empowered crew members. You have invested time and passion into the components of your plan, so entrusting it to a mediocre group of people is something you cannot afford to do. Instead, you must be committed to building and developing a successful Flight Crew.

Transforming a group into a team is one of the biggest challenges that business pilots face. You can try using any number of surveys, exercises, and analytical data, but nothing allows you to gauge the contributions of your team like observation. I work hands-on with my clients to continually peel all the layers back on performance, keeping a close eye on their team members' perceptions, intentions, and impact on the rest of the staff.

With the right tools (Chapter 4), you will identify team members who should be part of your crew; those who will support the team, the company, and the plan. You may realize that some will not. Identifying people who are focused only on themselves is sometimes an unfortunate reality. What do you do with those employees?

The answer can be a tough pill to swallow for most business pilots. But here's the good news. Never have I walked in and pointed out employees to terminate. Instead, we enhance the culture that provides the opportunity for engaged team members to step up and perform at the highest levels.

Disengaged team members tend to reveal their true intentions as you develop the environment that will support your plan. Often, some will move on as your culture enhances, rather than embracing it. Ultimately, you must develop a unifying culture; one that engages and empowers your team to produce the results needed for elevation.

Pilot's Log:
Invest the time needed to hire the right people to your culture; never waste time holding onto those who damage it.

PRESSURIZE THE CABIN

Flight Crew Development begins as you assess your current culture; the environment in which everything grows. How would you describe your culture? Is it unifying, empowering, inspiring? How would your team describe it? Taking a culture assessment is an important step in creating and protecting the environment needed for elevation.

In aviation, elevating to high levels is an essential step in the flight process and absolutely necessary to arrive at any destination. However, at altitudes of 12,500 feet above sea level, it becomes crucial to pressurize the cabin; the environment inside of the aircraft. To protect the crew and passengers from the issues incurred by the low air pressure outside of the aircraft, adjustments are required. Your business is no different.

Regardless of skill, no crew member is capable of surviving at high levels, in an aircraft with an unpressurized cabin. Is your environment prepared for a shift in pressure? As your business elevates, pay careful attention to your environment and the need to make adjustments to account for the changes in workload, duties, responsibilities, and accountability. Elevation requires change, and change requires adjustments.

Successful business pilots must be aware of anything, or anyone, who could damage their environment as their aircraft ascends. One disengaged team member can cause a small crack in the window, which can have significant effects regarding the safety of the entire flight.

Protect your crew by first focusing your attention on the environment they operate in. Assessing culture prior to take off is essential, but rarely completed. How can you determine if your cabin is ready for the pressure of elevation: the demands and stress associated with growth?

In my book, *The LEADERSHIP Connection*, I share with leaders that when the conditions are right, great growth occurs. To elevate, develop a unifying culture by using the Visionary Vowels. You can then foster a dynamic environment; pressurizing your cabin and protecting your engaged crew members during your flight.

Visionary Vowels:

A	Attitude
E	Excellence
I	Initiative
O	Outcome
U	Unwavering

Attitude - Your flight requires your crew to bring their "A" game every day. Your environment must be optimistic, positive, and upbeat regardless of the hazards encountered on the flight. Never settle for sub-par attitudes when you strive for above-par results.

Excellence - Good is not good enough, when GREAT is achievable. The success of your flight requires a crew dedicated to high levels of excellence, in every action they take.

Initiative - A Flight Crew that does what needs to be done without being told to do so is crucial in achieving the objectives in your plan. A passive approach prohibits elevation. Empower everyone to take initiative.

Outcome - Everything needs to serve a purpose as it relates to your Flight Plan. Leaders must have an outcome for each objective and goal. Outcomes provide the buy-in from each crew member for the actions required.

Unwavering - Business pilots will be tested; it comes with the territory. So they must possess an unwavering commitment to their flight plan and their crew. Stand strong on your belief levels.

When these five conditions are present, and at the right levels, leadership will grow and you and your crew will experience the optimum flight conditions for elevation. Use the Visionary Vowels as a gauge for culture, and gain a better understanding of the quality of your environment.

Use the chart below to assess your culture. With a scale of 1-10, 10 being the best, rank each Visionary Vowel, from your perspective. To gain greater insight, ask your leadership team and other team members to do the same, from their perspectives.

Culture Assessment

Visionary Vowel		Rank (1-10)
A	Attitude	_____
E	Excellence	_____
I	Initiative	_____
O	Outcome	_____
U	Unwavering	_____

With a possible score of 50, where did your culture rank? When assessing culture, most businesses return with an honest, realistic grade of 30-35. There is always room for growth and you must identify the necessary course-corrections to improve each one.

A low score is not a reflection on you as a leader, unless you are unwilling to make positive adjustments in your culture. Your score is a key indicator of untapped potential, and the importance of developing a unifying culture cannot be understated. In the Marine Corps, our culture was referred to as *esprit de Corps* (The Spirit of the Corps). Every Marine was expected to maintain the highest levels of esprit de Corps.

Pilot's Log:
Be brutally honest with yourself, and expect the same from the team members who also assess your culture.

FLIGHT CREW DEVELOPMENT

Will your cabin be pressurized as you elevate, or will the limitations of your culture prevent you and your crew from ascending higher? Business pilots make grave mistakes by not combining the optimum culture with the optimum Flight Crew. With a lackluster culture and a weak team, it is easy to feel the excitement of your plan fade away.

All too often, teams are loosely assembled, with the hope that someone's knowledge, or seniority, will make them a positive addition to their plan. Casually positioning your existing staff is not a viable solution. Each unique flight plan requires a Fight Crew; committed team members who fulfill the positions necessary to support your business aircraft as it elevates.

With a keen focus on your culture: your environment for growth, it is now time to identify and develop your Flight Crew. As exciting as it is to create the flight plan, it is always more exhilarating to develop the people supporting, implementing, and course-correcting it.

I have had the privilege of leading many teams, in multiple industries, to new levels of elevation. Critical to our success was my focus on finding the balance between experience and enthusiasm; prestige and passion; technique and talent. I used a simple formula for choosing my Flight Crew.

> **PEOPLE WITH PASSION**
> **+**
> **POSITIONS WITH PURPOSE**
> **=**
> **FLIGHT CREWS WITH ELEVATION**

At the media company, creating a visionary ecosystem to support the achievement of 300 percent annual revenue growth was just the first step. Protecting and guarding that environment, as we elevated, was paramount. Our culture provided the conditions necessary to support my leaders, help them to grow, and position them to achieve the elevation required for our flight plan.

Throughout the next three chapters, we will focus on the human factor; identifying and supporting people with passion, infusing each position with a deeper purpose, and developing Flight Crews with a foundation of leadership and vision, who are all striving to achieve greater results.

Your Aircrew:

1. Aviators
2. Flight Crew
3. Ground Support

Chapter 4-6 will also provide you with the leadership tools needed to build, develop, and stretch the vision of your entire crew as you *ELEVATE*. With the creation and development of your Aircrew, your Business Flight Plan will come to life.

Chapter 4

Business Aviators

Engage!

"Can you fly this plane and land it?" "Surely you can't be serious?" "I am serious. And don't call me Shirley." Leslie Nielsen delivered that hilariously memorable and often quoted response in the classic movie *Airplane!* The question remains relevant today for ambitious business leaders. Can you fly this plane and land it? Entrepreneurs ask themselves this question each day, while their teams ponder their possible answers.

While I did not start my career at the media company as a business pilot, I soon earned my way into the cockpit. Not only did I become an integral part of the Flight Crew, but I became the architect of our flight plan and discovered the importance of each position within our entire business.

Working my way from entry-level scheduler to vice president provided me the unique opportunity to support the flight plan from each level of leadership in our company. Like all aircraft, the cockpit crew is essential to successfully achieving elevation, but most businesses have empty seats for these positions. Surely, that does not make any sense.

I won't call you Shirley, but I will stress the importance of the crew members you allow to operate in the cockpit: your Aviators. With your plan in place, the members of this unique team take ownership of each component of the Flight Plan.

With a sharp focus on keeping your business on target, empowering your team members, and identifying your new leaders, being an Aviator takes tremendous discipline and dedication. The duties are understandably far different than the roles fulfilled by your other Flight Crew members.

AVIATORS

Like an aircraft, each business is unique in size, scope, and capabilities. Fortunately, all organizations require similar roles and responsibilities to *ELEVATE*. Your Aviators are typically comprised of your senior executive team, working together to develop and support the Flight Plan. They also offer their own insights and make contributions to strategic decisions.

In larger companies, this team commonly consists of the members from the "C" suite: chief executive officer (CEO), chief financial officer (CFO), chief information officer (CIO) and chief marketing officer (CMO). But these specific titles are not required of your Aviators. In fact, most small businesses may not have these exact positions. Instead, they may feature a president, vice president, and various director-levels of leadership.

In today's modern aviation, the aircraft cockpit crews consist of a captain and a first officer. Technology has since replaced the navigator position with GPS instruments, but the duties associated with someone focused specifically on the route have much merit for today's business flight plans.

Regulations do require that all modern aircraft are flown by a two-person crew consisting of a captain and a first officer; the co-pilot. The captain is the senior pilot, regarded as the "pilot in command". The pilot actively operates the controls of an aircraft while it is in flight and is ultimately responsible for arriving at the destination safely.

Stepping into the cockpit and sitting in the pilot's seat is not something to be taken lightly. Nor is the decision to appoint the members of this elite crew. Aviators must work together as a unit to achieve more than any individual member of their crew can do alone. They share duties to ensure a successful flight.

Business Aviators:

1. Pilots

2. Co-Pilots

3. Navigators

Pilots

"For some years, I have been afflicted with the belief that flight is possible to man." Three years after writing these words, Wilbur Wright and his brother Orville, put their belief level to the test and achieved elevation. On December 17, 1903, Orville piloted the first flight, lasting only 12 seconds. On the final flight, Wilbur took the controls and flew for 59 seconds.

Wilbur and Orville Wright sat in the pilot's seat before the word "cockpit" was even invented. On that day, history was made as both brothers followed their dreams and supported each step of the world's original flight plan. How strong is your belief level in your plan?

As the owner of a business, you may call yourself CEO, President, or Founder. Regardless of your title, you are the Pilot, responsible for elevating and arriving at your destination. To *ELEVATE*, you are permitted to call yourself the CEO, but not the Chief Executive Officer. Sitting in the pilot's seat, and preparing for take off, you become the Chief Engagement Officer.

A business leader's role becomes as multi-faceted as a business pilot. Regardless of the size of the company, you are the driving force; the fuel needed for elevation. You are the beacon of positivity, the deliverer of dynamic messages, and the setter of high expectations. You are the captain of consistency and camaraderie. Successful business pilots focus on 5 Aviator Essentials to guarantee a GREAT flight.

Aviator Essentials:

1. Set regular meetings to analyze the Flight Plan status

2. Engage the crew, creating a commitment to excellence

3. Hold the crew accountable for important data

4. Support and edify each member of the cockpit crew

5. Establish Rewards and Incentives for high-performers

Sitting in the pilot's seat is meant to be a rewarding experience, not a lonely one. A great co-pilot will share each of the Aviator Essentials with you.

Co-Pilots

In aviation, no co-pilot's job is simple. They show up early, obtain weather briefings, and share the aircraft duties with the pilot. They both perform the flying, preparing the cabin and passengers for landing, handling radio communications, and ensuring the flight plan is successfully completed.

Sitting directly next to their pilots, co-pilots are instrumental in providing a safe flight. They can be referred to as a flight officer or the first officer. Similarly, your business "co-pilot," is your second in command; your wingman/wingwoman; your go-to. Your co-pilot may very well be your key to high levels of elevation. In many companies I coach, I act as the co-pilot until one of the crew members has earned it.

Bill Gates, one of the wealthiest people on the planet, is the pilot for Microsoft. He fulfills the roles of Chairman and CEO, but has never been in the cockpit alone. Gates met his co-pilot, Paul Allen, at a private school. It was Allen who actually came up with the company's first name, "Micro-Soft." His belief in their Flight Plan was so strong that he convinced Gates to drop out of Harvard University to pilot their aircraft.

While their list of accomplishments is extensive, Allen spearheaded a deal for Microsoft to purchase a disk operating system (DOS), leading to a contract that would eventually run on IBM's PC line. This contract led to the success, wealth, and fame that Allen and Gates experienced. At one point, Microsoft was a small business, too. It is now worth over $250 billion.

As the vice president of the media company, I sat in the co-pilot's seat, but often assumed many duties for my pilot. I took complete ownership of the plan and the steps necessary to elevate. I worked directly with our Flight Crew and paid particular attention to developing the leaders in our crew, by focusing on assisting our pilot with the Aviator Essentials.

Pilot's Log:

Your co-pilot must exemplify the core values of your company, while being a driving force for your Flight Plan.

Navigators

Is business elevation possible with the combined efforts of a focused business pilot and co-pilot? Yes. But it is wise to enlist the support of dedicated crew members, as they step up to the challenges of growth and begin to present solutions for success. Remember Aviator Essential #2: *Engage the Crew at the Highest Levels of Excellence.*

As you *ELEVATE*, you will undoubtedly spark the entrepreneurial interests in other team members. Typically, at least one crew member will stand out as a potential Aviator and express their desire to enter the cockpit and support the flight plan at higher levels. This could be your Navigator.

Sharing the exclusive duties within the cockpit sends a direct message to the entire crew about your commitment to growth and your dedication to the team. At the media company, our navigator was our Media Director. Matt had his finger on the pulse of our technological media solutions, relevancy to our clients, and he was able to keep his eye on our Flight Plan.

As our navigator, Matt supported the efforts of the pilot and co-pilot, by helping to implement a training program that developed and transformed our team into the Flight Crew we needed. He also shared in the Aviator Essentials by monitoring our flight, advising the cockpit crew of possible delays, while ensuring that hazards were avoided. He had a keen awareness of our position at all times. But he was not our only navigator.

The navigators of a business flight ensure that systems and processes are maintained at the highest levels. But do not rush out to appoint a navigator. This position must be earned; never given. When the wrong team members participate at the executive level of elevation, you can experience disastrous results. Identify people who exhibit high levels of teamwork, believe in your company, and possess the ability to get the job done.

Pilot's Log:

Choosing a navigator requires pilots and co-pilots to enhance their leadership skills.

AVIATOR CONTROLS

Business Aviators share the common purpose of ensuring the success of the Flight Plan, which typically require an investment of additional hours. Rarely will your flight achieve new levels of success with a 9 to 5 work ethic, or as we said in the Corps, an "eight and skate." All Aviators must be willing to put in the extra time required for elevation.

In addition to fulfilling their other core responsibilities, Aviators must focus on the most important component in the plan: the development of their crew. In fact, properly building your team will help to buy back time as they take more initiative, get the job done right the first time, and collapse time frames on success. More on delegation, in Chapter 5.

Pilot's Log:
Business pilots must do more than design the plan; business pilots develop the team to carry it out.

Creating a plan is always easier than developing the team to carry it out. Aviators will not complete the flight alone. They need team participation to ensure the high levels of efficiency and effectiveness required for elevation. Without a laser-focused approach on developing the rest of the crew, it does not matter how GREAT your processes and systems are; what matters most is how GREAT the people are who run them.

As Business Aviators, we know the importance of focusing on our plan, but in regards to developing our crew, where do we start? There are two Aviator Controls to keep your hands on. These two handles allow you to hone your leadership skills, while simultaneously preparing your crew for flight.

Aviator Controls:

1. Teamwork
2. Team Tools

TEAMWORK

Different than running a company, Aviators strive to fly their business aircraft. We stretch ourselves, and our Flight Crews, to reach new levels of success and unexpected levels of discovery. The development of the crew is paramount. With the right levels of teamwork, Aviators can better utilize the tools and training needed to guide their entire team to their destination; not just faster, but better. Teamwork takes work!

In contrast to the high number of disengaged people, statistics show that the vast majority of employees want to be part of something special; something GREAT. This disconnect is clearly a leadership issue and Aviators often fail to make the adjustments necessary to fully engage their teams.

The Atlanta Journal Constitution performed a survey in 2015, polling thousands of employees on 19 specific statements. Asked which were most important, the number one statement was, "I feel genuinely appreciated at this company." Over 71 percent indicated that appreciation was a significant factor to them.

"People want to feel like they are a valuable part of something good," stated Jim Minnick, CEO and co-founder of the financial services firm eVestment. Below are the Top Five from the AJC survey:

1. 71% - Being appreciated
2. 71% - Belief that the company is going in the right direction
3. 65% - The company operates by strong values and ethics
4. 64% - Senior leaders understand what is happening
5. 63% - Things are done efficiently and well

Following the Top Five, was the the idea of feeling part of something larger than yourself, and that the job meets or exceeds their original expectations. Belonging to a team is a result of feeling part of something; owning a piece of the shared identity of the collective members. How often do you show your appreciation? As Aviators, we answer this question within the culture we develop.

One of my first clients with Think GREAT was the U.S. Marine Corps. Traveling to Iowa, I shared the concepts of my book, *The GOAL Formula*, with the Marines of Recruiting Station (RS) Des Moines. As part of their identity, this unit referred to themselves as the Wolf Pack, admiring the teamwork among wolves, and seeking to emulate that within their Marines.

With a personal invitation from the commanding officer, my wife and I later attended the Marine Corps Ball with the members of RS Des Moines. It was an amazing opportunity to be part of something special; something GREAT. During his opening speech, the Commanding Officer addressed his Marines and made a statement about their decision to call themselves members of the Wolf Pack. He proudly stated...

 Pilot's Log:
"The strength of the wolf is in the pack; the strength of the pack is in the wolf."

At the media company, we focused heavily on creating this level of teamwork. One of our first steps was to remove the word employee from everything. Our Employee Handbook became our Team Member Handbook. Employee Recognition programs became Team Member Recognition. No one was an employee. They were an important part of our team.

We did the exact same thing with our managers. We removed "manager" from as many titles as possible. Our Sales Manager became our Sales Director. Our Operations Manager and Assistant Manager became our Operations Director and Operations Supervisor. We needed our leaders to direct and supervise our crew, not manage them.

People in every industry talk about building strong teams, but few experience the results from creating true teamwork. In a team-oriented culture, each Aviator contributes to the overall success of the organization and the development of the individuals in the crew. Everyone benefits from teamwork through mutual support and an increased sense of accomplishment. Your crew will take on specific portions of your Flight Plan; the objectives and action items needed for elevation.

TEAM TOOLS

The benefits of building a team and achieving teamwork include higher levels of morale, increased collaboration, and a determination to find solutions. But Aviators cannot build teams by good intentions alone. They require tools to develop their crew; tools that allow them to grow in their roles as leaders, while empowering a new wave of leadership.

Empowering Business Pilot Tools:

1. Organizational Charts

2. Job Descriptions

3. Workflow Charts

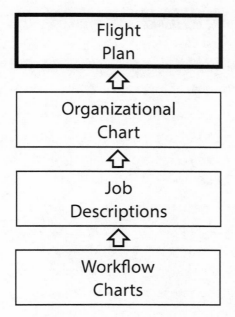

I know what you are thinking. Yes, these items do look familiar. When I meet with Business Pilots, those who are ready for take off, I ask to see their organizational charts, job descriptions, and workflow charts. Too often I am handed an incomplete set of documents, or nothing at all.

In most organizations these tools are merely afterthoughts, if the documents even exist. Those who have them completed have rarely transformed them from mere documents to the empowering tools necessary for Aviators to control and execute successful plans.

As an Aviator at the media company, these were living, breathing documents to me and our entire crew. They allowed us to keep our finger on the pulse of the most important factor in our business - the human factor.

Organizational Chart

Reporting to my first duty station, it was exciting to meet all of the Marines in my new unit. Not surprisingly, I was issued a copy of my direct chain of command. Complete with the names and ranks of the leaders above me, the list went all the way up to my Commander in Chief, Ronald Reagan.

In the military, chain of command is everything. It is the system that controls the actions, tasks, and logistics of each platoon, unit, battalion, or even an entire branch of service (Coast Guard, Army, Navy, Air Force, Marines). It is the positioning of the team to support the mission; the plan.

It is imperative to the success of our military that the chain of command is adhered to. It promotes the correct leadership to assure success and is the line of authority and responsibility along which orders are passed. It is also imperative in a successful business.

Your Organizational Chart is your chain of command, eliminating confusion with regards to position and purpose. It is your playbook: a visual representation of how your team needs to be positioned to best support your Flight Plan. Each plan requires course-corrections, adjustments, and tactical maneuvers, so Aviators must be willing and able to make the necessary enhancements to their teams at any point.

At the Media Company, I created and implemented over two dozen versions of our organizational charts during a period of just over seven years. Some had significant enhancements, while others were minor; all were relevant to our flight. At any given time we had a current organizational chart, which represented the actual team we had in place.

To achieve new flight levels, I also created the next version, and sometimes a third, based on our ascension rate to higher flight levels. Thinking ahead and designing our future organizational charts, we had the opportunity to visually map out the crew we needed at each flight level.

Business Aviators collaborate on new team members, promotions, and the new positions required for elevation. Having the ability to see your future crew, in the present, is a powerful tool indeed.

Below is a sample of a basic organizational chart from the media company.

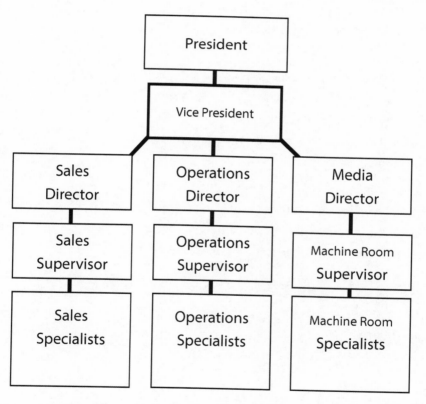

More than mere boxes on a sheet of paper, our organizational charts featured specific titles, and the names of each crew member. Every position served a specific purpose with regards to our plan, and our job descriptions captured that purpose, in addition to the duties.

Pilot's Log:

Use your organizational charts to position your current and future crews to support your Flight Plan.

Job Descriptions

To accomplish the countless military missions of our nation, over 7,000 jobs make up the five branches of our Armed Services. With lives on the line, there can be no confusion about what is expected from the team members within their ranks. The importance of providing clarity to each position cannot be understated.

Each service member fulfills a specific job, or in lengthy military terms, an MOS (Military Occupational Specialist). At the end of boot camp I was informed that my MOS would be 7311 (Seventy-Three Eleven). Nervously, I asked my drill instructor what that designation meant and he informed me, after a few colorful words that I cannot repeat here, that I would be, "Talking to aircraft".

I left his presence a bit confused, but thought twice about asking him again. I soon discovered that I would be trained as an Air Traffic Controller, working in the control tower and speaking to the pilots of the planes. The overview of my job description was crystal clear.

Air Traffic Controller: Air traffic controllers routinely perform various duties and tasks related to the control of air traffic and vehicles within the designated areas aboard an established airport control zone, expeditionary airfield or remote area landing site.

While I was trained as an air traffic controller, I was developed as a U.S. Marine. Taking the keen focus of purpose into the media company, I developed the job descriptions necessary to support our organizational chart. Each time our organizational chart adjusted, I ensured that our job descriptions reflected our new crew.

I have discovered that most companies fail to use any form of a job description. While some try, they often go overboard, detailing every possible action associated with that job. Regardless, the results are the same in both situations. Leaders rarely use job descriptions as empowering tools and team members remain unclear as to their full role.

I now assist clients by creating job descriptions that provide clarity, showing how the position supports the organizational chart, which supports the Flight Plan. I focus on a one-page tool of empowerment providing purpose, a list of essential duties, and the skills required to get the job done.

Position Overview

To unify our team, the first words of each job description were the same, "To help accomplish the sales goals by..." This was then followed with a deeper meaning of the position. We shared "why" this position exists. Provide purpose, not process, and you will engage and empower the person filling this position and striving to fulfill its purpose.

Essential Duties

Each job description should list about a dozen key responsibilities. Rather than a "To-Do List" of actions, these essential duties are required to develop a well-rounded crew member who is focused on growth and success. Essential duties allow leaders to identify the training required to achieve top performance, and through shared duties, can unify your team.

The #1 Essential Duty of each of our leaders was, "Lead by example". Each supervisor, director, executive, and c-level leader had this as their first duty. The #1 Essential Duty of each crew member was, "Have a sense of urgency". Each team member understood that this was the expectation.

Requirements

List the skills required to provide unparalleled excellence; leadership, technology, sales, customer service, education, etc. Again, avoid the "encyclopedia" style and stick with specifics.

On the next page is one version of my job description as the vice president of the media company.

VICE PRESIDENT

Position Overview

To help accomplish the sales goals by ensuring continued growth and upward mobility. To develop and maintain relationships that will perpetuate forward momentum and profitability. To ensure company-wide development to continually improve the skills of all SMV Team Members so they can guarantee the utmost in customer satisfaction. To ensure the security & protection of all client materials & information.

Essential Duties

- Lead by example
- Orchestrate – Delegate – Supervise
- Ensure that all orders are completed correctly and delivered on time
- Maintain a productive, professional, exciting environment focused on results
- Design and support the plan for exceeding company goals (Flight Plan)
- Responsible for implementing leadership development company-wide
- Lead sales meetings and leadership meetings
- Oversee the daily corporate operations
- Identify company reports for accountability
- Responsible for the termination of employment for team members
- Ensure that the company is compliant with all federal and state regulations
- Ensure that any and all updates to our systems are implemented

Requirements

Leadership: Meetings, Accountability, Development, Required Reading
Sales Skills: Sales Manual, Inside/Outside Sales, Industry Knowledge
HR: (Full Authority) Recruit, Hire, Reviews, Warnings, Termination
CRM Status: Super User
Technology: MS Office, Filemaker, Xytech, Illustrator, Photoshop

There was no more, no less. I still focused on my duties as an Aviator, developing the job descriptions for the entire crew as we elevated to 300% growth.

Workflow

The frustrations of errors, mistakes, and miscommunication lead to more than just frustrated team members. The impact can be costly, especially when it encourages customers to take their business elsewhere. This certainly does not help your flight to *ELEVATE*. Identifying how you do things correct and on-time is crucial.

Our systems at the media company detailed the processes linked together for success. But our workflow reflected how we performed each action to complete every order properly. With nearly thirty unique media services, we had a variety of steps required for success.

I tracked the bulk our mistakes to misunderstandings in how we processed business. I knew that we were capable of completing every media order flawlessly because we often did just that. But not often enough. Our workflow charts helped us in three ways.

The Benefits of Workflow Charts:

1. Identifies the correct steps for each process
2. Allows for reduced times for completion
3. Increases team member knowledge

One of my clients provides wall covering solutions, a unique architectural fusion material that wraps around doors, columns, and other surfaces to allow for new dynamic looks to existing areas. As I began working with their sales team, I discovered that the operations team often required two weeks to provide a project proposal. The objective was three days.

With two weeks to wait, many prospective customers went elsewhere, so I immediately looked at the workflow for their proposal process. As you may have guessed, it was not a formally developed tool, but rather a collection of "Here's how it should work" suggestions. The two week turn times caused frustrations for the sales team, the operations team, the customers, and the Business Aviators.

Speaking with the operations team, it became clear that they did not always receive the data needed from sales reps, for a fast turnaround time. I set up a session dedicated exclusively to proposals and we identified the necessary steps and information required for a three day turnaround.

Next, we compiled this information into the workflow, the steps for success. We then created a supporting tool for the sales reps, which allowed them to gather (find) the information and transition it to operations. It took about three weeks to lock down the workflow and the "Fact-Finder" to reduce turn times on proposals.

Within one week of implementing the new workflow, turn times had been reduced to one week. During the second week, the operations team began hitting the goal of three days and determined that they would soon be able to guarantee a two day turn time on proposals over the following week. They did it. It was always possible, but without the proper workflow, "Correct and On-Time" rarely arrived.

Building a workflow is possible for every action, regardless of the complexity. Below is a snapshot of our exact workflow for creating DVDs; a highly technical and detailed process that we made simple.

DVD Authoring

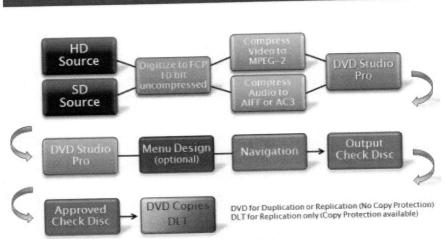

- Any editorial must be completed in FCP (see Offline/Online)
- All "Approved" check discs must have the "Check Disc Approval" form signed by the client
- For additional authoring options see Rate Sheet – Page 13

All of the steps in a defined workflow required an individual or department to be held accountable for its execution. Workflow charts are valuable and empowering tools that allow each crew member to develop a deeper understanding of how things work in your organization. Investing time in creating the proper workflow charts eliminates wasted time and allows the Aviators to train with a purpose; to increase efficiencies and effectiveness.

Workflow charts support the duties listed in the job descriptions; job descriptions support the positioning of the team on the organizational chart; organizational charts support your Flight Plan. See how this works?

AVIATOR PRIORITIES

There is a huge difference between training and development. I tend to focus on the higher law of "developing" the deeper people skills of leaders and the crew. Communication, inspiration, delegation, and motivation are all powerful development components. But training is different; much needed, but different.

Training serves a necessary purpose for Aviators. We train our teams to know more. With greater knowledge comes greater performance and results. Unfortunately, many team members waste costly hours in unnecessary or redundant trainings.

Every training session, course, or program must support the development of a Flight Crew that can contribute to the success of the flight plan. Training your team members on your workflow charts is a valuable use of time and resources. Aviators must communicate frequently with one another to ensure that all training is in alignment with the needs of their Flight Plan and the development requirements of their Flight Crew.

As Business Aviators, we step into the cockpit with the intention of flying our aircraft to new, exciting destinations. But it is ultimately our ability to develop our Flight Crew that will determine how much time we spend flying our plane versus fixing it.

Chapter 5

Business Flight Crew

Excel!

In 2015, Deloitte University published, *Global Human Capital Trends*, stating that "Culture and engagement is the most important issue companies face around the world. 87 percent of organizations cite culture and engagement as one of their top challenges, and 50 percent call the problem 'very important.'"

Business Aviators cannot afford to have culture and engagement fall into the category of "issues." The success of each flight plan depends on the ability to build, develop, and lead high-performance teams. "Team building" is not just another hot buzzword, it helps to unify your culture and increase engagement. But, many business leaders struggle with the strategies necessary to properly develop their teams.

It is typically a forgone conclusion that Business Aviators are going to enthusiastically support the Flight Plan. But to *ELEVATE* to higher levels, the engagement of the entire team is required and each level of leadership in your organization will play a vital role in your plan.

The idea of assembling a talented and results-oriented crew makes perfect sense to everyone. Pulling it off, however, is often met with challenges in most businesses. Stagnant, unmotivated employees are difficult to transform into dynamic crew members. Facing upwards of 72% disengagement, the thought of building a strong team can seem impossible.

Care and diligence must go into filling the positions required for elevation; determining the best individuals to board your flight and perform their duties. Premature promotions and hasty hirings can lead to instability within your ranks. Attempting to fill the spaces of an organizational chart, like you are checking off items on a To Do List, can be damaging.

As an Aviator, you must have your finger on the pulse of your Flight Crew. You are responsible for maintaining the culture required for elevation, which means that you are responsible for the rules and regulations; the policies and procedures that protect you, your team, and your company.

Understandably, this is not the most popular topic among Aviators. But ignoring it is not a viable option, nor is pushing it off to your HR department. When your mission, vision, and destination are important, you will not want your time, or the time of your Flight Crew, to be spent repeatedly dealing with bad behavior and unacceptable performances.

The Uniform Code of Military Justice (UCMJ) is the foundation of military law for every member of the armed services. Regardless of which branch you serve in, the UCMJ sets crystal clear expectations for the behavior of Marines, sailors, soldiers, and airmen. Below is an extremely short list of some of the topics covered in this military "Employee Handbook."

- Article 86:   Absence without leave (AWOL)
- Article 89:   Disrespect toward superior commissioned officer
- Article 92:   Failure to obey order or regulation
- Article 96:   Releasing prisoner without proper authority
- Article 99:   Misbehavior before the enemy
- Article 104:   Aiding the enemy
- Article 114:   Dueling
- Article 118:   Murder
- Article 122:   Robbery
- Article 123a: Making, drawing a check... without sufficient funds
- Article 126:   Arson
- Article 127:   Extortion
- Article 128:   Assault
- Article 129:   Burglary
- Article 132:   Fraud against the United States

For lesser offenses, Non-Judicial Punishment (NJP) is established and allows leaders to provide discipline on a smaller scale, typically within their own command (department). NJP punishments can range from reprimands and reduction in rank, to loss of pay and barracks confinement.

For larger violations of the UCMJ, court martials may occur. There are three types: Special, Summary, and General Court Martials. Depending on the severity of the offense, potential punishments can include confinement in the brig, dishonorable discharge, and even death.

Military leaders protect their environments by immediately addressing the smaller offenses as soon as they arise.

THE FOUR LAWS OF FLIGHT CREW DEVELOPMENT

Business owners start their companies with the idea of jumping into the pilot's seat, taking off on an amazing journey with their crew, and achieving the highest levels of success. Of course, everyone is going to be happy, grateful, and exhibit positive attitudes, right? Unfortunately, this scenario rarely happens. But it can.

If you are committed to elevating, you must take the development of your Flight Crew just as serious. Behavior issues will come up; they do in every company. But how you handle them will determine where you spend your time. Establishing and honoring the four laws of developing your team will position your entire crew for a safe, timely, and successful flight.

Four Laws of Flight Crew Development:

1. Establish high EXPECTATIONS
2. Provide timely EVALUATIONS
3. Ensure RECOGNITION for Positive Behavior
4. Deliver CONSEQUENCES for Negative Behavior

* Invest more time in steps 1-3 and spend less time in step 4.

1. Establish High EXPECTATIONS

When leaders fail to establish the boundaries for acceptable behavior they inadvertently create a culture that tolerates multiple levels of behaviors, and some can negatively impact their ability to *ELEVATE*. Establishing expectations is the responsibility of the Aviators, and fortunately, there are only two types you can set: high and low. But you must decide which one.

What happens when you set low expectations? That's an easy question to answer; your team may hit them. Setting high expectations is the only way to develop a crew focused on achieving high levels of elevation. But I have found that most Business Aviators ignore the smaller signs of bad behavior until they become major issues of disengagement.

Hoping that a problem will go away has never worked, and making this mistake will affect other members of the Flight Crew. Serving in the Marine Corps, I experienced an environment of very high expectations, and anything not covered in the UCMJ was established as part of our culture.

The expectations were high on everything from regulation haircuts to properly wearing our uniforms and spit-shining our boots. We arrived 15 minutes early to be considered on time. We stayed late to get the job done. Expectations were high and crystal clear. They were understood by all Marines, but even in the Corps they were not always followed by everyone.

In the civilian world, expectations are often not as clearly articulated and there can be varying levels of misunderstandings, resulting in unacceptable behaviors and poor performance. A leader who fails to establish expectations fails to build the foundation necessary for elevation.

Starting my job at the media company, I did not step into a culture of high expectations on personal performance. Everyone took pride in the technical capabilities we provided to our clients, but we were not always able to deliver, as many team members missed the mark on their performance.

During my first few weeks, I observed people showing up late, but recieving little more than a disappointed look from their supervisor. Others took extended breaks, leaving their co-workers shouldering heavy workloads. Again, no repercussions. Verbal warnings were rare and written warnings were nothing more than a mythical idea that "might" happen the "next time." Expectations were not high and poor results often followed.

Were policies and procedures available to our team? Yes, there was an employee handbook, which was rarely reviewed. Our team members received this "encyclopedia" of dos and don'ts when they were hired, and then it was promptly stored away, never again to be seen.

As a rising leader, I transformed our employee handbook into our Team Member Handbook. More than changing the title, I consolidated the rules and regulations into an informative and much shorter guide to match the high expectations on behavior and performance we needed for elevation.

Our handbook became a leadership tool. During the on-boarding process for new crew members, our leaders took time with their staff to share the purpose of our policies. Investing the time up front allowed us to avoid wasting time on the back end, dealing with problems. Your handbook should outline everything from PTO to notifying supervisors when they are sick. Leave no room for doubt on performance and behavior.

If you have tolerated certain behaviors, like tardiness, poor communication, and mediocre performance, it is fair to say that some team members may not be enthusiastic about new higher expectations. But most will embrace them, especially if they have continually witnessed bad behaviors being allowed in the past from others.

You must unify and become unwavering on the new expectations. Then, with other key leaders, collectively share the purpose behind the expectations to your entire crew. High expectations must serve the overall good of the team, the company, and the customer. Do not announce them then fail to bring them up again. Consistently discuss high expectations during meetings and other opportunities to communicate with your team.

Pilot's Log:

It is not always easy to roll out high expectations on personal performance, but it is always worth it.

2. Provide Timely EVALUATIONS

"When am I going to get my review?" is a question that many team members think about for far too long. Afraid to ask their leader, they harbor the negative feelings of being "forgotten" until they decide to share their situation with their co-workers. When a review fails to happen and the word gets out, it spreads like wildfire.

Rarely is the leader involved in that communication flow until it is too late. By this point, the failure to provide a timely evaluation has started a negative domino effect throughout your entire company and you have lost credibility with your team. But you may never know the extent.

Yes, timely evaluations are that important. One of the biggest complaints I receive when I interview team members is that their reviews are past due, or worse yet, never happen. Why? Most leaders say they are too busy. But many are not well-versed in how to deliver an empowering review, failing to see the benefit of this vitally important connection to their team members. Putting off reviews translates into your failure to meet the high expectations that your team has for you.

Equally as bad as ignoring an evaluation, many reviews happen only out of protocol, rather than out of purpose. Remember, high expectations have a purpose. 90 day reviews, or annual evaluations, become a mundane ritual that fails to empower the team member and becomes a source of "time consuming" annoyance for the leader.

Typically, most employees are paying attention in their reviews, with the hopes of hearing the word, "raise". While I am a huge fan of raises, I have always set a high expectation and understanding that they are based on performance; earned, never given.

A timely evaluation allows more than just an opportunity to discuss salary increases. Both the leader and the team member should collaborate together on enhancements, for both parties. So how do you provide a timely review that empowers your team members and your leaders?

Because reviews are so important, leave nothing to chance and schedule all of these sessions well in advance. For new team members, set the dates for their 90 day and annual reviews in their hiring paperwork. New team members and their supervisors, should receive a summary form on the first day, describing their position, pay rate, benefits, and their dates for their reviews; 90 day and annual.

For existing team members, including your leaders, have their annual reviews scheduled in your calendar. When promotions occurr, immediately set up monthly performance evaluations to support and guide them. Then set up 90 day reviews to fully assess their performance in their new roles, which may include a raise, based on performance.

Ok, so timing is important. But what needs to be discussed during an evaluation? GREAT question! One of the reasons that so much attention goes into developing job descriptions is because these are one of the tools for reviews. If you are not judging how well they fulfill the duties and responsibilities outlined for them then what are you reviewing them on?

In the reviews, invest time to discuss the crew member's purpose, as it is detailed in the "Position Overview" section of their job description. Next, address each bullet point in their "Essential Duties" to identify strengths, weaknesses, and discuss solutions for growth.

Create a formal "Performance Evaluation Form" which features a scale, ranging from 1-5 to assess their performance levels, 5 being best.

1. Unsatisfactory

2. Marginal

3. Needs Improvement

4. Meets Requirements

5. Exceptional

While the goal is to score as many 4s and 5s as possible, pay particular attention to anything under that. If a team member receives a 3 or below, the leader is required to give specific examples to ensure that both parties clearly understood the expectations set, and how to hit higher numbers for their next review.

Our performance evaluation went deeper into the behaviors of each team member, focusing on the soft skills necessary for higher levels of growth. Below is a sample of our Performance Evaluations, both for our team member reviews and leadership reviews.

Performance Evaluation - Team Member

Demonstrates Job Skills	1	2	3	(4)	5
Attendance	1	2	3	4	(5)
Team Communication and Teamwork	1	2	3	(4)	5
Client Communication	1	2	3	(4)	5
Organizing and Planning	1	(2)	3	4	5
Systems and Checkpoints	1	2	(3)	4	5
Attitude and Appearance	1	2	3	4	(5)
Taking Initiative	1	2	(3)	4	5

Performance Evaluation - Leader

Leads by Example	1	2	3	(4)	5
Creates High Levels of Morale	1	2	3	4	(5)
Fosters Teamwork	1	2	3	(4)	5
Inspires Collaboration	1	2	(3)	4	5
Supports the Flight Plan	1	2	3	(4)	5
Provides suggestions for growth	1	2	3	(4)	5
Communication Skills	1	2	3	(4)	5
Delegation Skills	1	(2)	3	4	5

While there were additional topics, including those that were relevant to our media industry, we focused on specific areas that would allow our Flight Crew and our leaders to develop at the highest levels, to best support our flight plan.

Timely evaluations are powerful steps that nip many weaknesses in the bud, before they become behavioral problems. Performance evaluations allow you to track and document any issues, which can keep you out of legal trouble if you need to fire or discipline a team member.

Timely evaluations should be an empowering activity for everyone involved. Your crew will know what is expected of them, and the feedback will allow leaders to address any issues, while providing team members the opportunity to correct their behavior. After all, that is the purpose of an evaluation, isn't it? To get better?

Pilot's Log:
Providing timely evaluations sends a positive message to your entire team that you care, not just about the flight plan, but about them.

3. Ensure RECOGNITION for Positive Behavior

Recognition shows appreciation for a job well done. Remember, the survey from The Atlanta Journal Constitution showed that 71% of team members ranked, "being appreciated" as the number one attribute they are looking for from their employer. Failing to recognize positive behavior only ensures that you miss this empowering opportunity as a leader.

Rewarding positive behavior leads to less time spent course-correcting bad behavior. Recognition is more fun than reprimanding, but leaders fail to dedicate more time to it. In many organizations, reprimands tend to happen more frequently than recognition.

Just as an overlooked review leaves people with the feeling of being forgotten, unrecognized positive behavior can have the same impact. Recognition needs to be infused into the DNA of your culture. But for many leaders, recognition often takes a back seat to their other duties, while it should be front and center.

Most U.S. Marines serve a tour of duty for four years, and I was no exception. I served from 1987 to 1991 and there were many forms of recognition during that time period. One in particular was for good behavior;

the Good Conduct Medal (GCM). Earned by serving a specified number of years without reprimands, it could be assumed that this medal would take four years to earn, especially with the Marine Corps' commitment to the highest levels of excellence.

The Marine Corps does not chase perfection. Instead, they strive for progress. The GCM is earned after three years of good conduct during a full tour of duty. I earned my GCM and I am grateful that it was not based on my entire four year tour. I needed to make progress during my first year.

In addition to this medal, Marines earn recognition by completing courses on personal and professional development. Exceptional behavior may also result in a Meritorious Mast. This written recognition of work well done is of greater value than a Letter of Appreciation or a Certificate of Commendation.

While the consequences for bad behavior were crystal clear, every attempt was made to consistently course correct our actions and recognize each Marine for our positive behavior. It was an integral part of Marine Corps culture. Is it an integral part of yours?

In my experience, team member recognition is scarce because leaders often struggle to understand how to provide inspiring forms of recognition. They think too narrowly, worrying about what people will find rewarding. Unfortunately, both parties are left feeling less than enthusiastic, even though positive behavior was exhibited by the team member.

The key is to establish your recognition based on your high expectations. When team members achieve excellence in their performance, recognize their efforts in front of other team members. By recognizing positive contributions to your flight, your crew will make more positive contributions.

At the media company, we provided two specific forms of recognition. Weekly, all of our leaders met to make nominations for our Team Member of the Month award. Each leader was required to make a recommendation from another department; not their own. This positioned our leaders to observe the behaviors in other departments and recognize those crew members.

After the meeting, the owner of the company would personally pass out recognition "coins" to team members who nominated that week. While there was no monetary value, there was great personal value. Each coin had inspirational phrases on them, such as, "Well Done," "GREAT Job," or "Amazing Work".

This weekly recognition encouraged other team members to take their performance to new levels. At the end of each month, the Team Member of the Month award was announced in front of our entire company. The winning crew member was acknowledged for supporting our flight plan and received a certificate and $100 cash.

This too became part of our culture and behaviors dramatically changed in a positive direction. After awhile, we struggled to pick a team member because so many were stepping up and delivering high performance efforts. What a GREAT problem to have.

An often-stated reason for overlooking recognition is time. But even leaders with the best of intentions will regret this mistake. Their failure to recognize positive behavior transforms into frustrations, complaints, and dissatisfaction. With these experiences, many team members hold back on their true potential. Leaders who ensure the recognition of positive behaviors ensure that untapped potential is unleashed.

Prioritize consistent recognition in your organization and you will create a productive and exciting environment. Authentically provide recognition as a way to say "thank you" for the efforts that support your flight plan. You will encourage more similar actions and position your entire flight for greater levels of elevation.

Pilot's Log:
Consistently recognizing positive behavior will influence other crew members to eliminate negative behavior.

4. Deliver CONSEQUENCES for Negative Behavior

Well, here we are... Step 4. Like most business pilots, I know what you may be thinking: delivering consequences is not fun. But it is a lot less fun dealing with bad behavior that runs amok, impacting your culture and team engagement. The time not invested in setting high expectations, providing timely evaluations, and ensuring the recognition of positive behavior may cause time to be redirected toward the dreaded "consequences".

If you have not yet developed the dream team, the Flight Crew needed to *ELEVATE*, you may be feeling the pinch from a lackluster team, or possibly a few team members without drive. Sometimes, just one person can taint the performance of the rest of the team.

Disciplining employees is a challenging and unpleasant part of leadership. But it is a necessary law that must be followed. Most leaders steer away from delivering consequences, which is why all leadership positions must be earned; never given. For your flight to be successful, all leaders must be able to perform their duties during the difficult situations, not just the fun ones.

At the media company, we focused heavily on steps 1-3 (expectations, evaluations, and recognition). We were consistent with all three, but unfortunately, some team members positioned us to deliver the consequences for their negative behavior.

For the good of the team, the company, and our flight plan, all of our leaders were on the same page; swift actions for bad behavior. While certain actions, such as theft, violence, or derogatory comments required immediate termination, most were minor violations of policies that required our leaders to properly course-correct our crew members.

We experienced everything from tardiness to workflow mistakes; from insubordination to poor client communication. We even had a supervisor place a DVD in our microwave oven, just to show others what would happen when you turned it on. While the lights and sparks emitted from the DVD were impressive to watch, a write-up helped to ensure that no one duplicated this bad behavior.

When steps 1-3 are consistent, receiving consequences for negative behavior should not come as a surprise to the team member or the supervisor. In addition, consistent communication helps to eliminate the uncomfortable confusion that can occur when employees are unaware of their leaders' dissatisfaction with their performance or behavior.

Timely evaluations are one valuable tool for minimizing the need for delivering consequences. Also, scheduling regular meetings with your crew will help to identify bad behaviors early on, allowing for additional course corrections. But when you identify an issue that is not getting resolved, you will be best served to have a plan in place for delivering consequences.

You may want to require each leader to take the necessary steps to resolve the issue, not necessarily to punish the team member. This may be challenging, but having the steps in place will make this process easier.

The Four Phases of Delivering Consequences:

1. Verbal Warning

2. Write-Up (1st)

3. Write-Up (2nd)

4. Termination

Verbal Warning:

Because the purpose of delivering consequences is to instruct, guide, and course correct, rather than to punish, I chose to begin with a *verbal warning*. In this meeting, I met with the team member who committed the violation and their supervisor. The verbal warning was not only a course correction for the team member, it was a training session for my leaders. I conducted the verbal warnings until they were comfortable to take over.

During the verbal warning, I asked if the team member was aware of our policy and reminded them that it was in our Team Member Handbook they had signed. I provided suggestions for improvement and asked if they had any questions or concerns. Because we tied their behavior into the welfare of the rest of the team and the company, most of our crew acknowledged their bad behavior and expressed the desire to improve.

I let them know that the verbal warning required no signature from them, but would be documented in their file. I also stated that the next step would be a *write-up*, if they could not make the necessary improvements. I firmly reiterated that we wanted each team member to succeed with us.

Write-Up:

If bad behavior continued, a formal *write-up* followed. With this step, we re-discussed the suggestions for improvement and identified any issues that prevented the resolution of the issue. More than a punishment, we attempted to find solutions that would help the crew member to get back on track.

Both the team member and their supervisor signed the write-up document, which stated that the next violation would result in another write-up. The team member received a copy of the write-up and the original was filed. After the meeting, I would re-group with the supervisor to identify other ways we could support our crew member.

In addition to the write-up, additional consequences could range from a movement in their shift time to a denial for a raise, from disqualification for a promotion to a lateral move to another department.

If the same behavior was repeated, a second write-up occurred. Again, the behavior was documented and signed, and additional consequences may have been implemented, such as going home for the day or the week without pay. At this point, close attention was always paid to offer support to course correct.

Termination:

In all of my years of leading teams, there was never a termination that did not keep me up the night before. Even when team members bring the entire circumstance on themselves, firing someone is typically awkward and uncomfortable. But leaders are required to do what is right for the entire crew and for the success of the Flight Plan, even if it means letting someone go. Welcome to the cockpit.

Terminations can be risky if you do not follow the right steps. Failure to provide previously documented warnings could land you in court on a claim of wrongful termination. Always consult with your HR department or consultant to ensure that all steps, policies, and procedures are followed to the "T".

Most leaders do not enjoy firing people and most people do not like being fired. More than just an emotional and financial strain, it is a sign that something went wrong. There was a disconnect; a missing link between that team member and your core values, goals, culture, mission, vision, destination, or a number of any other factors within your company that were tolerated, perhaps for too long.

While terminations can be uncomfortable, there is usually a sigh of relief from the rest of the crew when bad behavior exits the business aircraft. It is not uncommon for many other team members to experience the impact of bad behavior by their co-workers.

By focusing on expectations, evaluations, and recognition, you will minimize the delivery of consequences. But if a termination is required, you can sleep soundly at night by following the four phases of delivering consequences.

Pilot's Log:
Invest time on the front end of team welfare, rather than wasting time on the back end, after it brings down your flight.

DELIVERING THE SPARK

Your Flight Crew is assembled, and now it is time to unify your people and expand their efforts. Creating business synergy will position your crew to do more than maintain your aircrft, it will help everyone to work together in unique ways to lift your flight into the wild blue yonder.

Chapter 6

Business Synergy

High Performance Jet Fuel.

The final members of your Flight Crew step aboard your aircraft and the door slowly closes. Excited to take flight, a thought runs through your head and you ask yourself, "Did I forget anything?" You wonder if it is enough to have the right people in the right positions. Elevation does not happen by having the right people in your aircraft. Elevation occurs when you assemble your Flight Crew and bring them together with synergy.

Teams need to be unified; brought together for a greater purpose. More than teamwork, you need *Synergistic Teamwork* to *ELEVATE*. That sounds GREAT, but what is synergy and how can you harness it to power your flight? To achieve something, it makes sense that you should be able to define it. The Merriam-Webster dictionary defines synergy as:

> noun syn·er·gy \'si-nər-jē\
> *The increased effectiveness that results when two or more people (or departments) work together; combined action.*

Synergy is another hot buzzword for today's business pilots. So popular, that it falls into the top 10% of words searched on the Merriam-Webster website. In the top 1% - *leadership*. Starting to see a trend? Leadership is the engine for your business aircraft and synergy is the fuel; the leader's ability to bring people together and dynamically combine their efforts into the flight plan.

Business Synergy is the creation of a whole that is greater than the sum of its parts, and it can be infused into your culture by controlling time. Although controlling time sounds challenging and time-consuming, it really is not. In fact, you have tons of time to work with. Most of it, however, is probably dedicated to ineffective activities; uncontrolled time. But we can change (enhance) that.

SYNERGY TIME

Making the assumption that a great team will naturally achieve great results is a mistake that is often repeated by anxious Aviators. The right people, in the right seats, without synergy, merely means that you have your positions filled now, with better people than those who occupied them before. That does not guarantee success, and you need a guarantee.

Assembling and developing a successful Flight Crew takes time and dedication. But amassing a talented group of people is not your outcome; synergy among your crew is your outcome. It cannot be ordered or forced, but it can be achieved through inspiration and focus. Synergy thrives in the right environments, but the wrong conditions will diminish its potential.

Growing up in Southern California, I have always been a fan of the Los Angeles Lakers. In the 1980s, I watched the "Showtime" Lakers, marveling at the skills of Magic Johnson, Kareem Abdul Jabar, James Worthy, and Kurt Rambis. Seeing them win the championship titles in 1980, 1982, 1985, 1987, 1988 was exciting. It would be easy to say that winning a championship is a forgone conclusion when you have champions on your team.

Their pilot, head coach Pat Riley, did not take the abilities of his assembled team for granted. He harnessed the combined power of their efforts and instilled in each player that, "The difference between success and winning is in a person's attitude," not just with their skills. His coaching style created the synergy needed to win the final four titles in that era.

Fast forward to 1997. The Lakers' head coach, Del Harris, acquired 18-year-old Kobe Bryant and 24-year-old Shaquille O'Neal. Even with these two skilled players positioned on his roster, he was unable to create the synergy needed to unify the team and secure a championship. Fired in 1999, he was replaced by Phil Jackson.

With the same superstars, Coach Jackson stepped into the cockpit and elevated the Lakers to championship titles in 2000, 2001, and 2002. Winning three-in-a-row is not an easy accomplishment. In the 70-year history of the National Basketball Association, this feat has only been accomplished 5 times. Coach Jackson has been responsible for three of the five.

The Lakers' "three-peat" was the result of synergy, not just skill. Coach Jackson did more than assemble his players; he transformed them, getting them to sacrifice their personal statistics for the greater good of the entire team. He did not settle for having the right players in the right seats. He aspired to achieve elevation with synergy.

Pilot's Log:
Without synergy, even championship players will fail.

BUSINESS SYNERGY

Flight Crew Development is called *development* for a reason. Rarely do you ever build the perfect team. In fact, you never do. It takes time to unify your crew and develop synergy. While it may be easier to see how synergy can positively affect the results of a sports team, it is equally important in the workplace, supporting every component of your flight plan.

Business Synergy fosters high-levels of teamwork required to produce an overall better result than if the members of the Flight Crew worked individually toward the same objectives. As your crew becomes more cohesive, their capabilities are impacted in a number of positive ways.

The Benefits of Business Synergy:

1. Purposeful interaction between team members increases

2. Meaningful communication improves

3. Common goals are established and accomplished

4. Overall satisfaction grows - customers and team

5. Bonds develop that guard against hazards (coming in Part 3)

At the media company, we needed more than teamwork to accomplish our lofty goals. We needed synergy to make the long-term impact required for high levels of elevation. With synergy, our environment changed and we began to develop camaraderie; one of the things I desperately searched for after leaving the Marine Corps.

The dictionary may define camaraderie as "A feeling of good friendship among the people in a group," but it means much more when you serve in the military. With lives on the line, camaraderie is more than friendship; it is the essence of what binds us together. It links each individual in the team and provides everyone with the cohesiveness needed to function as a collective unit. Camaraderie is the pinnacle of a team's strength.

This can certainly be achieved in the civilian world. Even in the absence of gathering in war rooms, ready rooms, foxholes, and tranches, camaraderie will thrive in the right corporate environment. Teams with shared values, commitments, and sacrifices, will begin to develop a deep bond as they connect through Synergetic Teamwork and strive to accomplish the goals and objectives in the Flight Plan.

Pilot's Log:
You will know when camaraderie occurs; not by seeing it, but by feeling it.

Stepping into a client's environment for the first time, I search for signs of teamwork and camaraderie. Unfortunately, both are typically absent or at extremely low levels. But not for a lack of wanting. Most Business Aviators see the benefit of using the high-octane "fuel" of synergy to engage their team members and *ELEVATE* their flights.

Creating the jet fuel required to ignite your business engines is an important step. But where do you start? What if I told you that the elements of that fuel are right at your finger tips? To achieve business synergy and create the combustion necessary for elevation, you must buy back a simple commodity called time.

BUY BACK TIME

A team is at its strongest when the members are gathered. So it is only natural that leaders focus on bringing their team members together. Typically this event is referred to as a "meeting." Oh yeah, the dreaded meeting. While they should lead to great results, they are often a source of frustration in most organizations. They are also a high-volume storage tank of "time." You will now have the access code to unlock that storage unit.

Usually perceived as a waste of time, I receive the same defeated look from employees when I ask about the meetings in their companies. During my one-on-one discussions and group sessions, even most leaders list meetings in the "improvements needed" section of their plans. When team members express their frustrations over the amount of meetings, I understand what they want is less time-wasting, pointless gatherings.

When people attend high-energy, inspiring, motivating meetings that are laser-focused on results, no one leaves saying, "Let's have less meetings." If your team is saying, "We need less meetings," it's a good indicator that your meetings have gone into the storage unit.

Getting team members together is vitally important to the success of an elevating business. But instead, most "business gatherings" leave people frustrated and disengaged. According to MeetingKing, an online resource firm, there are "11 million formal business meetings each day in the U.S. and we waste $37 Billion in unnecessary meetings every year."

Additional statistics from MeetingKing:

- Employees spend 37% of their time in meetings
- Leaders attend more than 60 meetings per month
- 47% consider too many meetings the biggest waste of time
- 39% admitted to dozing off during a meeting
- Over 70% brought other work to meetings

According to Atlassian, a software company based in San Francisco, nearly 31 hours per month are wasted in meetings, per employee. Research has found that the more meetings employees attend, the more exhausted they feel and the higher they perceive their workload to be. Are you starting to see where disengagement begins?

How much time do your meetings waste? How much do your meetings cost your organization? Bad meetings are often the largest expense you will never see on your P&L. You may be asking yourself, "Why do leaders continue to allow sub-par meetings to occur?" The most common response I receive is, "We have always had this meeting." Let's take a closer look at the devastating cost of bad meetings.

Without taking into consideration all of the additional expenses incurred from having employees (taxes, fees, insurance), we will simply focus on the cost of bad meetings, based on annual salaries. For the ease of math, let's focus on a staff of twenty people, with an average salary of $50,000. Your annual base payroll is $1,000,000. When your crew spends (or wastes) 37% of their time in bad meetings you will spend (or waste) $370,000 per year. What line item do you use to list that expense in you budget?

Worse yet, these bad meetings have an impact on the remaining 63% of their time. The negative effect is catastrophic, and there is an epidemic of these gatherings in the workplace today. Unless you make the commitment to control time, by establishing GREAT meetings, you cannot expect to *ELEVATE*. It is time to break the cycle of bad meetings and unlock the storage unit that is holding the time needed to create synergy.

GREAT MEETINGS

Ironically, over 90% of the attendees surveyed value meetings as an opportunity to contribute to the organization. Most people see the potential of powerful meetings but lack the ability to implement them. Are you ready to buy back the time you are already paying for, and reallocate it into the creation of Synergistic Teamwork?

As part of my client coaching sessions, I observe meetings. I attend sales meetings, staff meetings, project meetings, and even "emergency" meetings, as problems arise in their organizations. I participate in manager meetings, leadership meetings, and executive board meetings. Meetings, meetings, and more meetings. Tons of time, just waiting to be converted into the jet fuel needed for your engines.

I regularly witness the pitfalls of good intentions during their meetings. Wait, "good intentions" sounds like a good thing. Without clear focus and proper execution, even good intentions can produce bad results. Hence, lackluster meetings are typically the result of noble ideas. But these unsatisfying gatherings become breeding grounds for more disengagement.

To grow your company, you need empowering, exciting, collaborative sessions dedicated to elevation. Your objective is to have your team members leave each session better than when they arrived. If you want them to contribute to the growth and success of your organization, make the commitment to develop your crew, not just load them up with more information.

When all the layers are peeled off, most meetings are little more than glorified (and expensive) info-exchanges. "This is how we share information," is a common excuse for ongoing meetings that produce few positive results. Data is vitally important to exchange, but could your meetings achieve a higher level of impact? Yes, especially if they focus on more than data!

With your systems and accountability in place (Chapter 2), your regular status reports will eliminate the need for most of your "info-exchange" gatherings and you can begin to schedule the meetings necessary for elevation. GREAT meetings result in high levels of morale which positions your Flight Crew for more success.

Meetings are also platforms for developing all of your current and next-wave leaders, resulting in ongoing Flight Crew development and higher levels of elevation. GREAT meetings do not happen by chance; they happen by choice. I have found that GREAT meetings are the result of combining four specific elements.

The Four Elements of a GREAT Meeting:

- Purpose
- Outcome
- Actions
- Timelines

If you do not have these four elements identified, then ask yourself this question, "What are we meeting about?" If the answer is to exchange-information, then you are stacking more time into the storage unit. Synergy is not achieved as a result of exchanging data; it is achieved when there is a purpose, striving for an outcome, taking action, and meeting timelines. Without these four elements, you merely have another meeting.

Purpose:

The first question I ask my clients is, "What is the purpose of this meeting?" If they cannot answer this initial question, I encourage them to consider eliminating the meeting. Your purpose should include supporting and developing your Flight Crew, through collaboration. How does this sales meeting, staff meeting, or project meeting support the flight plan? The greater purpose of every meeting is to create synergy.

Outcome:

Each meeting should identify specific objectives to accomplish. If your purpose is to support the flight plan, then each meeting should target key areas, such as Q1 goals. If your purpose includes Flight Crew development, then allocate time to develop their skills by allowing them to conduct a portion of the meeting.

Actions:

Each meeting should identify actions, the additional steps that will support the flight plan. Is training required? Does a problem need to be resolved? Is a new product or service needed? What actions need to be taken to keep the flight en route? Identify them collectively with your crew, as you work collaboratively to find solutions.

Timelines:

Each action identified needs to have a timeline set for completion. Some actions may require less than a week to complete, while others may need more than a month. Timelines keep everyone focused and on track. At your next GREAT meeting, provide follow-up from the timelines set. Were they hit or missed? Course-correct as necessary.

Pilot's Log:

Strive for synergy: the joint work and collaborative environment found in GREAT meetings.

As Aviators, it is up to us to position our crews for success. We cannot expect to *ELEVATE* when our team is attending meetings that do not serve the greater purpose of our organizations and our flight plans.

PREPARING FOR GREAT MEETINGS

The ability to develop a successful Flight Crew is jeopardized when 37% of their time is occupied in unproductive meetings. It is a cost that businesses cannot afford. This is your opportunity to reallocate "time" into the right activities, and there is an abundance of time, ready to be unloaded from the storage unit of disengagement.

If you want your crew to benefit from synergy, an agenda is essential to keeping your meetings on track. In addition to over 90% of people seeing the value in meetings, 73% consider having a prepared agenda as "very important".

GREAT meetings are the training grounds for leadership. This is where the Aviators and the crew discuss the strategies and techniques necessary for achieving new flight levels. In sports, each winning coach spends more time with the players at practice (meetings) then at the actual games.

Practice, to a championship team, is everything. And yes, there is an agenda for each practice. It is that important.

For Business Aviators, a meeting agenda will ensure that purpose, outcome, actions, and timelines are met. It will also allow Aviators to control the quality of each meeting, by ensuring that four criteria are met.

The Criteria of a GREAT Meeting:

- Earned Attendance
- Destination Updates
- Sharing the Podium
- On Time - Every Time

Regardless of the GREAT meeting I was conducting (sales, leadership, operations, projects), I made sure that each criteria was understood and met.

Earned Attendance:

Attendance in your meetings must be earned, never given. Each attendee should serve a purpose in the meeting. Otherwise, why are you paying for them to be there? Nothing kills a meeting faster than a disengaged team member who keeps looking at their watch.

Be selective and allow only team members who bring their "A" games to attend your meetings. It is ok to shrink meeting attendance down then build it back up as enthusiasm and participation increases.

Destination Updates:

Start each meeting off with "Here's where we are." If you are on-track with your flight, share success stories. If you need course-correction to get back en route, open up the dialogue for solutions. Discussing your vision, mission, and core values at the beginning sets the tone for the entire meeting. While there will always be varying levels of information shared at meetings, sharing destination updates will make sure that the data is relevant.

Sharing the Podium:

"Sharing the Podium" is a concept that provides the greatest strides in Flight Crew development. Meetings should never become "One-man shows." If you plan on developing the skills of your Flight Crew, do more than just ask them to attend a meeting, encourage them to participate.

More than having them speak, enlist their help to prepare specific sections of the meeting and list them on the agenda. Allow them to grow by providing them with opportunities to participate at higher levels. Move your team members from spectators to players by having them train on key concepts and solutions.

For me, I considered a meeting GREAT when I was the spectator. I left better than I arrived, when my Flight Crew led an empowering, exciting, collaborative session dedicated to elevation. Share the podium to develop synergy.

On Time - Every Time:

Without an agenda, bad meetings become longer bad meetings. "Going over" drains everyone's energy and cuts into the schedules of those attending. You can immediately begin to enhance your team's perception about meetings by beginning and ending them on time. While this may be a new habit to practice, it establishes a respect for time. You, the leader, control time. If you cannot start and stop a meeting on time, the middle loses its meaning.

Regardless if you make it through the entire agenda, just stop on time. Rarely is there a topic so important that it validates the disruption of everyone's schedules. If you are not able to stay on time, reevaluate your agenda and make the enhancements necessary to be more efficient. This is a perfect time to enlist the support of your Flight Crew and allow them to contribute to the agenda.

Pilot's Log:

GREAT meetings lead to GREAT results.

DEVELOPING A SYNERGESTIC TEAM

Synergy is the power behind your flight. As an Aviator, combining and leveraging the skills of your Flight Crew will position you for the greatest return on your investments, efforts, and passion. By reallocating the time stock-piled in the storage unit, you will begin to energize your Flight Crew.

While synergy is mutually beneficial for the entire team, not everyone may embrace it at first. GREAT meetings are not always welcomed with open arms, but unwavering leaders will ensure that consistent, GREAT meetings take a foothold in your organization.

Business Aviators must always be prepared to share the importance of building a synergistic team. They must also be on the constant lookout for people who want to be part of that team. Just like a sports coach, you may be required to make "trades" to ensure that the right Flight Crew is positioned on your aircraft.

I turned on the TV and watched the Lakers celebrate their 2000 championship win, in the streets of LA. As the team gathered, each of the 15 champions expressed high levels energy, excitement, and enthusiasm. It was inspiring. Phil Jackson had a championship team. But he did not leave anything to chance as he prepared for next season; their next flight level.

The following year, the Lakers stepped onto the court with six new team members. Coach Jackson replaced 40% of his championship team. After winning another title that year, he did it again. This time, he replaced five team members; one-third of his team. While you may not be required to replace 30%-40% of your staff, are you prepared to make the "trades" necessary to maintain synergy and *ELEVATE* your flight?

Business Aviators must constantly be the "scouts" for their organizations, keeping their focus on the abilities of their team members. Are they using their skills at the highest levels? Are they contributing to the synergy required for elevation? Even with a successful crew in place, you cannot afford to stop developing your Flight Crew. You cannot leave anything to chance. To safeguard against complacency, use two keys to unlock future potential.

RECRUITING AND RETENTION

There is always room for improvement, if you are looking for it. The keys to maintaining a synergistic team are recruiting and retention. As the vice president of the media company, I ensured that recruiting and retention were constantly in motion.

Recruiting:

The success of your organization will be the ability of the Business Aviators to discover new talent. Hiring people is both an art and a science. By using your job descriptions as hiring tools, you can set the clear requirements in terms of skills. But your ability to share your vision will attract the right people to the destination of your organization.

Even when all of our positions, detailed on our organizational chart, were filled with the right people, we were searching for the next GREAT addition to our crew. Recruiting, in most organizations is reactionary, filling a position when someone quits or is fired.

Successful Business Aviators make recruiting proactive. It is not necessarily synonymous with hiring. Recruiting is the constant outreach for identifying future team members. Make it part of your plan. In addition to searching for new people, it also sends a message to your crew that you are in the hunt. Always be prepared to make the trades necessary to your roster.

Take the time necessary to find the right Flight Crew members. In addition to skill, look for people who are good communicators, those who could help to unite your team and work on your flight plan, positively and successfully. Also look for people with high levels of character, those who fit into your culture, through integrity and passion. I would take enthusiasm over experience in a heartbeat, .

Because Flight Crew Development is crucial, search for people who are coachable; people who want to grow and develop. Ask many questions during the interview process, positioning the person to tell you about their goals, their career objectives, and the things that they are looking for in a company and in their leaders.

But the most important question you should ask is, "How do you feel about being part of a team?" Their answers may range from, "Good" to "I love being part of a team. Teamwork is everything to me." Their reaction to this question can tell you a lot about them and make your decision easier. If you want to benefit from leading a Synergistic Team, find people who want to be a contributing member of that team.

Retention:

Doing a great job of retention, will cause less time in "reactive" recruiting. Retaining your dynamic Flight Crew members is a huge objective. The cost of replacing team members can range from 200%-300% of their annual salary, once you factor in all of the training you have poured into them.

Getting new team members up to speed takes time, so maintaining your crew is paramount. I have discovered that most people leave an organization, on their own accord, for one of two reasons. When I speak to those who feel the need to work somewhere else, they typically state the reason for leaving is, "Poor management and/or a lack of opportunities."

In all of my years of leading teams and coaching people, I have never heard anyone tell me their reasons for leaving were, "Strong leadership and an abundance of opportunities." To retain your team, become a strong leader, one who translates business growth into team member opportunities.

People are more willing to follow leaders who constantly share their destination with them. Even if the career opportunities are further down the road, do not forget that your retention ratios will go up as you provide the opportunity to be part of something unique; something GREAT.

Recruiting is actually another powerful tool for retention. Why? Because the best way to retain your high performers is to surround them with other high performs. Consistent recruiting efforts is a positive sign to your top crew members and allows you to replace your low perfomers. Recruiting positions you for success and increases your retention levels.

CONSTANT PERSONAL COMMUNICATION

There is too much at stake to remove the human factor from your flight plan, and it is ill-advised to strive for high levels of Flight Crew Development through e-mails and texts alone. I stayed in the loop with my Flight Crew through CPC (Constant Personal Communication). CPC will position your entire crew to reap significant benefits.

The Benefits of Flight Crew Development:

- Attracts skilled crew members
- Instills a synergistic mindset in your culture
- Reduces turnover
- Provides opportunities for gains
- Increases ability to navigate hazards (next chapter)

Flight Crew Development allows your entire crew to work together; grow together; In a heartbeat, together. It takes a commitment on the part of the Business Aviators, but is always worth the investment of time. Regularly connect with your team, not just your leaders, and ask for feedback about how people are working together and the challenges they face.

Stepping into the cockpit, assembling your Flight Crew, and infusing your entire team with synergy will allow your flight to achieve high levels of elevation. Unlimited amounts of potential will be unleashed from your team, and applied to the success of your flight plan, especially as you and your crew strive to avoid hazards by making *Tactical Maneuvers*.

Part III

Tactical Maneuvers

When everything seems to be going against you, remember that the airplane takes off against the wind, not with it.

~ Henry Ford

Part III

Tactical Maneuvers

Hazard Avoidance.

With a detailed Flight Plan in place and a synergistic Flight Crew ready for take-off, the only option now is to get your plane moving, right? But what about the hazards ahead? Hazards? What hazards? We all want, or at least hope, to experience ideal flying conditions. But that is rarely the case. Each business flight faces challenges, and Aviators must be prepared to navigate through a storm of issues, problems and less-than-ideal situations, if they expect their Flight Plan to be a success.

While some business pilots excitedly jump into the cockpit and attempt to take flight, with little regard for the dangers ahead, others are paralyzed by fear. Instead of facing their challenges head on, they remain motionless. As you can imagine, both techniques are ineffective strategies.

Just 23 years after the Wright brothers took flight, the Air Commerce Act was established in 1926, requiring pilots and aircraft to be examined and licensed. This act provided the establishment of safety rules and navigation aids, and ensured that accidents were to be properly investigated.

Born from the misfortunes of past flights, aviation safety encompasses the prevention of aircraft failures, through regulation, education, and training. It helps pilots and their crew members to make better decisions regarding the circumstances they face during their flights, both internally and externally. Fortunately, aviation safety is applicable in the business world, too.

With the proper understanding of the challenges that may arise, successful business pilots not only understand their circumstances, but they learn how to tactically maneuver to avoid negative implications within their organization. As a business pilot, you must not only be aware of the hazards that await, but have the courage to address them head-on with your team.

QUICK THINKING

Waiting for perfect flying conditions only results in delayed flights. Issues exist in your organization right now, some small and some large; some tangible and some intangible. Each can have a significant impact on your flight if left to chance. But they should not prevent you from elevating. Because some issues can rise without warning, being prepared is crucial.

An Airbus 320 is a commercial aircraft capable of carrying over 150 passengers and weighing over 90,000 pounds. On January 15, 2009, US Airways Flight 1549, made an emergency water landing, with the engines unpowered, in the Hudson River. The plane was the victim of a bird strike, impacted multiple times by geese.

The birds caused both jet engines to fail on the Airbus 320, yet each goose weighed only 15 pounds. These unannounced, small hazards immobilized an aircraft weighing nearly 50 tons. Captain Chesley "Sully" Sullenberger and First Officer Jeffrey Skiles, made the quick decision to maneuver, landing in the Hudson River and saving all 155 passengers and crew.

The incident is known as the "Miracle on the Hudson" and the story is being turned into a feature film by director Clint Eastwood. While there may have been no way to eliminate the threat of the bird strike, Captain Sullenberger and his crew were hailed as heroes because of their ability to take the actions necessary to maneuver and guide their aircraft to safety.

After 30 years of service, Sullenberger retired on March 3, 2010. His final flight, US Airways Flight Number 1167, reunited him with co-pilot Jeff Skiles and a half dozen of the passengers from Flight 1549. Sullenberger is now an international speaker and advocate for aviation safety.

Pilot's Log:
Even the smallest objects can have a major impact on the ability for your business to elevate.

Your business flight may never suffer from a bird strike, but how you handle your own unique challenges will be beneficial when they arise.

DECISIVENESS

GREAT Business Aviators are not developed during the smooth flights; they are forged during the challenging ones. A Business Aviator's legacy is defined by his or her resolve. Just like "drag" to an aircraft, flight hazards can constantly pull businesses down, damaging the morale of the crew and impeding the success of the flight.

Tactical maneuvering allows all types of hazards to be dealt with swiftly and appropriately, because they do not merely go away on their own. Business leaders must exhibit strong decision-making skills when faced with undesirable circumstances. They must be decisive.

One of the fourteen leadership traits of the United States Marine Corps is *decisiveness*. Defined by the Marines, "Decisiveness means that you are able to make good decisions without delay." I have found that most people make decisions intuitively (without rational thought or proof) rather than analytically (by using comprehensive review or discussion).

Are you and your Flight Crew exhibiting decisiveness when handling your current challenges? As a corporal in the Marine Corps, I was taught to "Make sound and timely decisions". The Handbook for Marine NCOs (Non Commissioned Officers) provides the following advice for being decisive:

> *To make a sound decision, you should know your mission, what you are capable of doing to accomplish it, what means you have to accomplish it, and what possible impediments or obstacles exist that might stand in the way.*

Often taught as the best defense, awareness of your circumstances removes the possibility of issues becoming threats. Aviation pilots must acknowledge all possible hazards and prepare for them. To ignore them would be foolish, and perhaps fatal. Business pilots cannot turn away from the issues they face either.

In aviation, basic fighter maneuvers (BFM) are tactical movements used to gain a positional advantage over a challenging situation. While you may never be in an aerial "dog-fight," the success of your flight will be increased by the awareness of potential hazards. As a business pilot, you must effectively maneuver, sometimes with little advanced notice.

Pilot's Log:
The worst decision is indecision.

EXPECTATIONS

Working with a wide-array of business types and sizes, it is always easy to gather a list of issues. During a typical SWOT analysis (Strengths, Weaknesses, Opportunities, and Threats), most employees have no problem filling up the "weaknesses" column with multiple problems.

Issues and problems could realistically be placed in the opportunities column, as their solutions provide immense opportunity for the entire team to grow, and for the organization to become better. To *ELEVATE*, you will need more than a list of weaknesses.

Unresolved issues and problems endanger your flight as they place unnecessary wear-and-tear on your aircraft, and additional stress on your crew. The rarely-used "Suggestion Box," gathers anonymous feedback for improvements, but is usually a failed exercise at fixing things.

At the media company, I did not want an ongoing, never-ending list of complaints. Anyone can tell you what they think is wrong, especially your disengaged team members. For a successful flight, you are looking for the enhancements required to allow your business aircraft to soar to new levels. Instead of asking for a list of issues, I encouraged my team to provide the formula for enhancements: two solutions for each issue.

1 Issue + 2 Solutions = Flight Enhancements

By asking for two possible solutions with each issue, team members are able to put more thought into the resolution of each hazard, and be better prepared to share their ideas, collaboratively, with other members of the Flight Crew. Remember, most meetings are forums for discussing what went wrong. But with GREAT meetings, you and your crew can discover solutions, make enhancements, and discuss what goes right.

In addition to asking for improvements, it was imperative that our entire Flight Crew understood what constituted an issue. Like the emergency room of a hospital, all types of incidents arrive. People have different understandings of what qualifies as an emergency. Everything from stubbed toes, to broken bones and heart attacks come through the same doors.

Fortunately, hospital staff is trained to prioritize every "emergency" they face. The same must hold true with your Flight Crew. Some people will treat a "stubbed toe" work issue, like a corporate "heart attack". Others will take the same "heart attack" situation and try to walk it off, like a "stubbed toe."

Both tactics are detrimental to the well-being of your business, and Aviators must decisively resolve hazards immediately as they develop. Thousands of unique variables intertwine to form the challenges facing businesses, but there are two main hazards that require tactical maneuvers.

The Two Hazards of Business Flight:

1. **Tangible Obstacles**   - Issues you see
2. **Intangible Turbulence** - Issues you cannot see

As a coach, I have witnessed more wasted time, frustrations, and missed opportunities due to the smallest hazards. Ignoring the challenges in your path only leads to increased turnover, unnecessary headaches, and sleepless nights. You cannot afford to ignore the situations that will affect your flight. Decisiveness will allow you to avoid their negative impact and confidently navigate through any situation.

Now it is time to get your plane moving. It's time to *ELEVATE*.

Chapter 7

Tangible Obstacles

Seeing the Issues in Front of You.

If you have children you are already aware of the "Invisible Issue Syndrome". Defying the laws of human biology and science, children, especially teenagers (and many husbands) possess the keen ability to be near issues, also known as chores, without noticing them. Most who suffer from this phenomenon easily walk by their clothes on the floor, dirty dishes in the sink, and trash in the yard without so much as flinching.

Acknowledging the issues could quickly translate into work, so ignorance is a common technique, while secretly hoping that mom will eventually make it all go away. Unfortunately, I often observe the invisible issue syndrome with many business pilots. Expecting mom to resolve your problems is not a recommended strategy, nor is it productive for the business to have the Aviators taking on the crew's overlooked chores.

Even sharp, savvy corporate executives are often guilty of failing to face the issues directly in front of them. Every business pilot is aware that hazards threaten their aircraft. But some try to handle them like an ostrich, burying their heads in the sand and hoping they pass. But they do not pass. Ironically, the ostrich is the largest bird that is not capable of flying.

Imagine being a bird and never being able to use your wings to soar. Imagine being a business pilot and never being able to use your aircraft wings to soar. That is what happens when challenges are perceived as chores and are ignored. Issues provide the personal development that Aviators require to become great leaders. It pays to reassess how you view challenges and the vast opportunity of growth they provide.

During my first three months at the media company, I discovered many issues, large and small. We had started to resolve some of the hazards in our path by streamlining a few steps in our workflow and launching a disclaimer for certain video formats, providing our clients a better understanding of the limitations of their media elements. It also reduced many returns, which was GREAT for our margins.

But our hazards did not miraculously disappear with a few minor adjustments. Failing to deliver a media order correct, and on-time had a significant impact on our clients' production schedules, air dates, and deliveries. While some clients patiently allowed us to correct our mistakes, others were not as cordial.

When an unhappy customer showed up with an incorrect order, most of our team steered clear. But these were exactly the opportunities I wanted. A tangible obstacle was being brought to our attention, sometimes rudely and unpleasantly, but nevertheless, it was put right in front of us to solve.

This was my opportunity to step in as the point person and step up to resolve it. Typically, the mistakes caught by our customers were the results of unresolved issues within our own company. Being the catalyst for solutions led to my three promotions, including vice president.

Pilot's Log:
Unresolved issues not only impact your crew, they filter out to your customers, impacting your bottom line.

THE VOLUME OF BUSINESS ISSUES

The inability to maneuver around your obstacles, or eliminate them completely, is due to two things. Either a business pilot chooses to ignore the issues, or they lack an understanding of the solutions. Obstacles must become a priority. Keeping a close watch on anything that can cause your flight to lose elevation is paramount.

Remaining in the cabins of their business aircraft, leaders lose their tactical advantage of identifying obstacles that pose a threat to their businesses. But I get it, they are busy running their business. Or perhaps busy dealing with the side effects of unresolved obstacles? Failing to survey their flight path, from the vantage point in the cockpit, business pilots jeopardize the success of their flight, allowing issues to repeatedly impact their team members and customers.

Awareness of your hazards is a start, but far different than resolution. This becomes clearly evident by making a quick search at Google.com. While writing this paragraph, I just performed a search for "Business Issues" and 1,260,000,000 results immediately popped up. Over one billion! That's a lot of problems being discussed. Remember the SWOT analysis? Employees can quickly fill up the weaknesses column with issues.

It is fair to say that no one enjoys working with ongoing, lingering challenges. By using the "one issue + two solutions" formula, from the previous chapter, it would make sense that there must be over two billion results for "Business Solutions". Unfortunately, only 86,000,000 appeared. That's million, not billion. Solutions are a mere drop in the bucket when compared to the one billion additional results found for issues.

The online search gap between the obstacles facing businesses and their solutions is a ratio that is mirrored in many companies. People seem eager to discuss what is wrong, but neglect the dialogue to discover the tactical maneuvers needed to course correct and get back on the right path.

This also supports why many business pilots have become masters at working with the multitude of challenges facing their flights. Rather than ignoring them, they now tolerate them. Understanding and resolving your tangible obstacles will improve your entire flight.

Statistics show that for every customer who files a complaint, at least 25 others have remained silent. Be grateful for complaints, as long as you are striving for solutions. Business pilots and their Flight Crew cannot expect customers to tolerate issues for very long. When they go to your competitor, your aircraft is hit twice from the same obstacle.

FOD - FOREIGN OBJECT DEBRIS

In the aviation world, how damaging can debris be? They can not only be costly, they can be deadly. As an air traffic controller, I was trained to be aware of the hazards facing pilots, but I was also expected to find solutions. In the control tower, we constantly scanned the airfield, identifying any possible objects in the path of the aircraft. We looked for other planes and helicopters, vehicles, or any objects large enough for us to see.

Working ten stories up, we could not possibly be expected to find everything that could threaten an aircraft. Most importantly, it is usually the smallest objects that have the largest impact. Before each morning shift, other airfield staff engaged in finding smaller obstacles. Members of the airfield crew performed shoulder-to-shoulder walks of the runways, searching for FOD (Foreign Object Debris).

According to Boeing, "FOD is any object that does not belong in or near airplanes and, as a result, can injure airport or airline personnel and damage airplanes." It includes any object that can be harmful to equipment, aircraft, airfield vehicles, and people. FOD can include pavement fragments, tools, maintenance materials, luggage, rocks, and pieces of other aircraft.

On March 26, 2007, a Bombardier Learjet 36A took off from Newport News/Williamsburg International Airport in Virginia. A crew member heard a loud "pop" and the takeoff was aborted. The aircraft was forced to perform a hard landing, blowing its tires. Rocks and pieces of metal were discovered on the runway after the accident. This FOD was overlooked.

On July 25, 2000, Air France Flight 4590 crashed at Charles de Gaulle Airport near Paris. The high speed Concorde encountered a piece of titanium debris on the runway, which fell off a Continental Airlines DC-10 that had taken off a few minutes earlier. 100 passengers, nine crew members, and four people on the ground died that day due to a small obstacle.

In addition to endangering lives, FOD damage has a high financial cost. It is estimated that these tangible obstacles cost the aviation industry over $4 billion a year. Needless to say, airports and airlines go to great lengths to minimize the costly consequence of FOD. What lengths do you go to?

BUSINESS FOD

How much does FOD cost your business each year? What tangible objects do you need to maneuver around or remove from your path? While FOD seems easy to identify in aviation terms, hazardous business objects also exist. Modifying Boeing's definition slightly, business FOD is "Any object that does not belong in or near your business and, as a result, can impact your ability to take off and *ELEVATE*."

Too many business pilots invalidate the impact that small obstacles have on their organizations. In a culture of tolerating issues, the lines are often blurred between real challenges presented by your Flight Crew and the mundane complaints filed from disengaged team members. In these environments, many business pilots are guilty of treating all issues the same, instructing their team members to "just work through things". As an air traffic controller, I never encouraged pilots to, "Just taxi over the FOD".

It is imperative to remove the small objects that could have a big impact on your performance and results. Our business FOD included equipment, resources, inventory, chairs, compensation plans, CRM (not using it to its full potential), systems, documents, tools, schedules, hardware and software, products, services, pricing, our sales pipeline, phone system, and dress code. And the list could go on.

The obstacles we faced at the media company were not unique to our team. Our competitors faced the same challenges. In fact, businesses outside of our industry also faced similar challenges. But focusing on the tactical maneuvers necessary to solve these problems, we increases our ability to grow by over 300%.

Ignoring your tangible obstacles is not a tactical maneuver. It contributes only to a dismal culture and a less-than-positive customer experience.

Pilot's Log:
Identify and remove any business FOD that can negatively impact your flight.

FOD PREVENTION

Most companies are plagued with business FOD, and they commonly steer off of the runway before gaining enough momentum for flight. Afraid to initiate take off, these pilots consistently guide their aircraft around the airfield, but go nowhere.

Anxious to *ELEVATE*, my clients are open to resolving their issues, even though prior attempts were not as fruitful as they had hoped. While they successfully created a long laundry-list of issues, their planes circled the airfield, resolving nothing. As their issues rose again, to a point of high frustration, the list was re-created, and again, no solutions were implemented. This cycle can leave a lasting negative impression on your team.

But there is a way to prevent FOD from damaging your business aircraft and hindering your flight. Working in the trenches with my clients and their teams, I have the opportunity to work with the obstacles holding their aircraft back. Typically their small issues present big threats.

Team members are often disenchanted at the idea of resolving ongoing issues, feeling that the cycle is going to start once again. Team members share everything from "We tried this before," to "Here we go again." Presented with a list of obstacles, owners may feel that they "cannot afford to fix everything." But they cannot not afford to leave the issues alone.

There is a way to break the cycle and empower business avaitors to perform the tactical manuevers needed to make real enhancements. Just like an airport, FOD control is most effective when focused on four main areas.

FOD Prevention Program:
1. Obstacles
2. Solutions
3. Implementation
4. Inspection

Page 146 and 147 feature the FOD List and the FOD Prevention Form.

Obstacles

On the FOD List, detail any obstacle in your path. This is a GREAT form to distribute to the team to get their initial thoughts on what they feel is an obstacle. It's important to let them know that you will soon be seeking two solutions for each obstacle they list. While some team members may need more than one sheet, it is in your best interest to identify every real obstacle in your path.

While gathering input from the entire team is valuable, it will be the Aviators and key Flight Crew members who determine what is a true obstacle; something that presents danger to the flight. Each individual obstacle identified then needs to be added on its own FOD Prevention Form.

Solutions

Once the Obstacle has been listed on the FOD Prevention Form, Aviators and Key Crew Members must strive to identify at least two solutions. Circle back with your team members, especially those who listed that particular obstacle and enlist their help to determine how to tactically maneuver around the obstacle, or remove it completely.

Implementation

Because people rarely welcome change, even positive change, the implementation must be properly communicated to the entire team, in terms of the importance of the solutions and timelines necessary for success. If phases are necessary to carry out the enhancements, each step in the phases should be detailed. Also, the appropriate training must be established to support the enhancements about to be made.

Inspection

Careful monitoring of the FOD Prevention process is essential to determine its success and measure its impact. Keep your team informed about the progress and the results, which will increase their buy-in and let them know that the leadership team is serious about removing obstacles. Consistently re-visit the obstacle and the solution to guarantee flight safety.

ELEVATE

FOD List

Tangible Obstacles in Our Flight Path:

Obstacle 1:

Obstacle 2:

Obstacle 3:

Obstacle 4:

Obstacle 5:

Obstacle 6:

Obstacle 7:

Obstacle 8:

Obstacle 9:

Obstacle 10:

Obstacle 11:

Obstacle 12:

ELEVATE

FOD Prevention Form

Obstacle:

Solution #1:

Solution #2:

Implementation:

Inspection:

THE RULE OF THREE

One of the primary reasons I am hired as a business coach is to continually identify solutions. An elevating business does not mean moving permanently past all of the issues and problems. Elevating means that you and your crew are capable of tactically maneuvering and handling the new, sometimes more complex, obstacles that will arise.

Every organization, from small businesses and large corporations, to non-profits, experience challenges at new flight levels. Growing businesses experience growing pains, which usher in new obstacles. Business Aviators can easily become overwhelmed in the vast stratosphere of challenges that are constantly presented.

This is likely a reason that very few obstacles have been removed from your flight path in the past. But the past is exactly that. The future of your success can now be based on a powerful principle I learned in the Marine Corps. *The Rule of Three* is a basic concept that gave me control over the obstacles at the media company, and allowed me to focus on the solutions.

The success of the United States Marine Corps is built upon developing an extremely efficient and effective fighting force. Marines have discovered how to make the best of any situation; how to tactically maneuver and handle obstacles. In their 115-page manual, *Warfighting*, Marines describe their process for efficiency.

Through years of trial and error, they have narrowed down what works and what does not work in challenging circumstances. From this, The Rule of Three was born. It stresses that each Marine should focus on three tasks, no more no less. Anything less is unchallenging and anything more is inefficient.

According to the NY Times, "The world assigns the number three elevated status." Their article, *The Power of Three* states, "Three claims will persuade, but four (or more) will trigger skepticism, and reverse an initially positive impression." It goes on to say that, "Three events going the same way three times in a row cause people to believe they are observing a streak." It's time for your team to witness a winning streak of solutions.

FOD SQUAD

Tactically maneuvering around hundreds of tangible obstacles is impractical, so where do you start? You start with three. Successful Aviators are able to prioritize their obstacles in threes, enhancing their ability, and the ability of their crew to remember and retain information.

At the media company, I put together a FOD Squad, key leaders dedicated to identifying and removing FOD. To start, we identified the three easiest, most simple obstacles and utilized our FOD Prevention Form to eliminate these issues. This simultaneously developed buy-in from the team as they finally witnessed solutions taking hold.

As a crew, we made three decisive maneuvers to resolve lingering issues. An Opening and Closing Checklist was implemented to ensure that our facility began the day and ended it with everything in place. We adjusted our shift schedules to provide better coverage and we updated our pricing guides to ensure that incoming calls were handled better.

Of course, we inspected each of these solutions with regular "walk-throughs" of our facility. We quickly tackled a few of the immediate, smaller obstacles and let our team experience the results of their input.

The U.S. Federal Aviation Administration (FAA) requires a daily inspection of areas designated for airplane maneuvering, and the removal of FOD. Your FOD Prevention Plan should focus on the top three current obstacles that need to be navigated.

Begin to turn your weaknesses into strengths and everyone benefits. According to Lee Resources, 91% of unhappy customers will not willingly do business with you again. But, 70% are more likely to do business with you if the issue is resolved in their favor. Be prepared to make the tactical maneuvers necessary for providing solutions and unhappy customers will be a thing of the past, too.

Dealing with the obstacles you can see is important, but to successfully navigate in your airspace, you must use these skills to maneuver through the unseen hazards that lie ahead - *Intangible Turbulence*.

Chapter 8

Intangible Turbulence

Feeling the Issues Around You.

Dream locations are filled with sandy beaches, 5-star hotels, and post-card-worthy views. The thought of arriving at an amazing destination provides an adrenalin rush of sheer excitement. You are 100% ready for a life-changing experience, but you need to get there first. Although considered to be the safest mode of travel, most people experience some level of anxiety about flying.

Anxiety typically causes a physical reaction, as positive feelings can be sent into a downward tailspin by the thought of motion sickness or being uncomfortably stuck in-between two strangers for hours. Some travelers, however, feel more than just anxious. They exhibit a psychological reaction called fear. A distinct phobia, the fear of flying is a often referred to as aerophobia or flight phobia.

The fear of flying can prohibit people from visiting great destinations as it intertwines with other phobias, such as being in closed spaces (claustrophobia), heights (acrophobia), and having a panic attack while being in places where escape can be difficult (agoraphobia). Ultimately, most people are not afraid of flying; they are afraid of crashing.

Business pilots also experience anxiety and fear and can easily miss out on the destinations they desire. Understandably, many are afraid to crash their business aircraft. Like most people, they rarely associate their fear of flying to the tangible obstacles (FOD) that pose a threat to their planes, like rocks on the runway or a flock of birds flying above the airfield.

Anxiety and fear are different and are typically associated with the intangibles, the unseen hazards. We have all been comfortably leaning back in our seats and trying to catch a little sleep when the plane abruptly shakes and feels like it's falling to the ground. The cabin fills with loud gasps from the passengers as they hold on for dear life. Hitting a small pocket of turbulence can be life-changing, at least during the few moments when it occurs. Flying into pockets of business turbulence can have a similar impact, but unfortunately, they have the potential of lasting much longer.

AIR TURBULENCE

No one has ever seen turbulence, but it is the most common fear expressed by nervous fliers. When an unexpected jolt happens over 35,000 feet up, it can send heart rates rocketing, spill beverages, knock over serving carts, and cause the unfortunate use of "barf" bags.

How dangerous is the largest fear of fliers? If the reactions of those onboard reflect their encounters, one would easily assume that turbulence is catastrophic. Most describe their encounters as "It felt like the plane was going to rip apart," and "We dropped thousands of feet in just seconds." But can turbulence actually cause planes to plummet to earth?

Everything from weather conditions, clouds, and jet streams can lead to disruptions in the air. But the most common form is called Clear Air Turbulence (CAT), which is caused when bodies of air meet but are moving at different speeds. As might be expected, there are no visual cues to alert pilots of this phenomenon.

Around the world, the aviation community shares a common classification of turbulence: light, moderate, and severe. Fortunately, the vast majority of turbulence encountered, approximately 99%, falls under light or moderate, bearing no risk to planes or passengers.

Ordinarily, it is an inconvenience to passengers and crew, not a major safety issue. Although some injuries happen each year, they are rare. Just like a bump in the road, which is common while driving a car, air turbulence is an expected part of flying. But what about the severe conditions?

Engineers design aircraft to handle significant amounts of pressure, testing them to meet stress limits for positive and negative G-forces. Even severe turbulence may only cause a loss of altitude of 40 feet or less, not the thousands that are often perceived. Airline pilot, and founder of www. askthepilot.com, Patrick Smith says, "The level of turbulence required to dislodge an engine or bend a wing is something even the most frequent flyer, or pilot for that matter, won't experience in a lifetime of traveling."

So how do Aviators deal with turbulence? The most common way is direct communication. Air traffic controllers and Aviators regularly share reports of air turbulence, allowing other pilots to prepare their crew and passengers for the encounter. Pilots may also slightly adjust their route, if needed, to provide a more comfortable flight.

The turbulence that will impact your business needs to be handled in the same manner, with crystal-clear communication and appropriate actions.

BUSINESS TURBULENCE

Removing the tangible obstacles from your path makes sense. Taking care of faulty equipment, replenishing inventory, and making adjustments to your systems will eliminate the business FOD covering your runway, allowing for a successful take off. But there also exists another, unseen issue facing Aviators - business turbulence.

Business plans never discuss feelings, emotions, attitudes, and egos, but they exist. The negative side of these intangible attributes can potentially create severe turbulence for you and your crew. I have seen them prevent business flights from launching, completely taking them off course, or worse yet, having them stall in mid-flight.

"People" issues, often referred to as "drama," pose the highest levels of anxiety, and often fear, among business pilots. "Light" cases of business turbulence can quickly escalate to "severe" if ignored. This type of disruption is not detectable on radar and we cannot accurately forecast when it will hit. But we can prepare for it and navigate better by having a clear understanding of how to identify and resolve it.

Business turbulence is caused by team members who do not support the Flight Plan - unintentionally or intentionally. They fail to share your passion and vision, or may have lost their excitement about reaching the desired destination. Sub-par behavior, reflected in their actions and dialogue, sends waves of negativity throughout your Flight Crew, threatens your aircraft, and damages your reputation as a leader, if unresolved.

People who disrupt business flights are often referred to as "toxic" or "cancerous," as they tend to destroy organizations from within. I prefer to think of them as *turbulent*. Like bodies of air, they are moving at different speeds than the rest of your crew. When they meet... instant turbulence.

It can often feel like turbulent crew members are ripping your plane apart, or causing it to drop from the sky, even with a "light" encounter. Why are these behaviors tolerated? Most people dislike confrontations, so many business pilots try every possible way of avoiding confrontational encounters, instead of bringing them to the forefront and addressing them with direct communication.

These issues should have been identified when you were assembling your Flight Crew (Chapter 5), right? Yes, in many cases you would make the necessary adjustments at this point. As you ELEVATE, you and your crew will raise the bar on performance, which may reveal the weaknesses in some team members that were once hidden or overlooked when your aircraft was grounded.

In the air, turbulent behavior is magnified and felt by everyone onboard. Plagued by fear, most Business Aviators allow turbulent crew members to either remain in their positions for years, or they unsuccessfully transfer them to other departments where the disruptive behavior rises again.

Moving the names on your Organizational Chart is not a viable navigation skill for dealing with this type of hazard. Turbulent people are typically not bad people. They may have lost the alignment required to be a member of your crew, but before you sharpen your "firing" axe too quickly, understand that most are salvageable with the right leadership and culture.

Pilot's Log:
The largest impact of turbulence occurs when you are not prepared for it.

NAVIGATING CONFLICTS

When I begin working with a new client, we focus on taking their business to the next level. We invest time in goal-setting, planning, and implementing their Flight Plans. We also focus on developing the tools necessary for elevation. But inevitably, we allocate time to resolving the conflicts that have caused extensive drag to their aircraft.

Regardless of the industry you are in (banking, construction, retail, etc.), you are in the people business. Your crew needs leaders who understand how to navigate personal and professional issues before they become complex hazards.

Because unacceptable behaviors are more prominent when higher expectations are established, it should not be surprising when some conflict arises during your flight. Developing the resolution skills of your Aviators is important because conflict is a natural part of human interaction.

Dealing with conflict, however, is far more challenging than removing the FOD that lies in your path, so most business pilots ignore this hazard as their first defense. But facing it directly is the only solution. Just like the aviation community, business pilots can utilize the same scale to identify the intensity of the turbulence they encounter from their crew.

Levels of Business Turbulence:

1. Light   - Professional issues at work

2. Moderate   - Personal issues at work

3. Severe   - Creating issues at work

Light - Professional Issues at Work

One of the most common issues that teams encounter is professionalism, or the lack of it. Rarely taught, it is typically assumed that people should understand how to conduct themselves with respect to the organization's culture. But some do not, lacking tact in their communication skills, not adhering to the proper dress code, or circumnavigating the systems.

A lack of professionalism causes people with good intentions to experience bad results as they unintentionally create conflicts with other team members and departments. Failure to address it head-on only allows this behavior to develop into bad patterns and habits, deepening the conflicts.

Anxiety and fear can cause business pilots to ignore conflict, incorrectly hoping that their crew members will increase their professionalism by observing others. If uncorrected, this turbulence escalates and eventually impacts customers.

Professional issues can come in all flavors. Below are common ones that can lead to conflict. Do any sound familiar?

Showing up late	Long breaks
Poor communication	Not getting the job done
Bad attitude	Lack of teamwork
No follow-through	Ignoring policies

Professionalism was expected at the highest levels in the Marines. We were constantly taught the proper way to represent ourselves and our Corps. Everything from haircuts to hand salutes, to inspections and flag etiquette was covered. Someone who exhibited a lack of professionalism, or "conduct unbecoming of a Marine," received immediate attention and course-correction.

The interaction was not only to reprimand the Marine, it was to guide and prevent future conflicts. Professionalism must be linked to your flight plan, which allows you to hold your team accountable and navigate the issues immediately before turbulence rises.

Pilot's Log:
Use performance reviews with your team members as opportunities to discuss increasing their professionalism.

Moderate - Personal Issues at Work

I completely understand what it is like to have personal issues while trying to maintain a job. I was employed in the media industry for three of Gina's four bouts with cancer, and it was not easy. I used all of my PTO and sometimes needed to leave work early, or show up late. But I handled each situation with professionalism, not wanting to disrupt our flight or crew.

Having a personal issue is not an issue, until it is brought into the work environment and begins to impact other team members. When someone's circumstances affects their performance and the performance of other crew members, unnecessary conflicts are created.

Immediate action is required, but most business pilots would rather push the "Eject" button, on their own seat, rather than being involved in these types of problems. There is a fine line to walk with Moderate Business Turbulence. When not handled correctly, personal issues that enter the workplace can take your flight well off course.

Below are common personal issues that can become turbulent and lead to conflicts. I am sure that some of below examples sound too familiar:

Car troubles	Health problems
Marriage problems	Legal challenges
Babysitter issues	Financial hardships

Most of us believe that emotions should be left at the door, but some people share all of life's challenges with their co-workers, even while they are still on the clock. Witnessing actions like non-stop personal phone calls and texting can cause some of your other team members to become frustrated; not necessarily at the person, but at the leader who fails to act.

You are not a psychologist or a counselor, so you are not expected to fix their personal issues, but you are expected to resolve the conflicts they are having before it damages the work environment. Instead of offering solutions to personal problems, strive for balance; help team members maintain their jobs through the challenges they face.

By using constant personal communication (CPC), successful Aviators become aware of potential conflicts early, setting up discussions with team members and their supervisors. I have always found it easiest to start by pointing out that their actions are beginning to affect their work and are impacting their co-workers. I attempt to work with the team member to resolve the issue at hand, asking them for their insights on possible solutions.

For the personal issues that continue and become hazards at work, remember to receive guidance from your HR department or HR consultants. If the team member continues to bring in their personal issues, revisit **The Four Phases of Delivering Consequences**: Verbal Warning, 1st Write-Up, 2nd Write-Up, and Termination.

Dealing with the impact of a team member's personal issues is one of the most challenging situations we face as leaders. Moderate turbulence requires you to exhibit compassion, focus, and professionalism simultaneously. Create an environment where you would fire someone because they could not control their personal issues at work.

Pilot's Log:
Great leaders preserve a person's dignity while maintaining the environment that others deserve to work in.

Severe - Creating Issues at Work

Spending nearly one-third of our adult lives at work, issues can have a significant impact on our team. "Light" professional issues and "moderate" personal issues provide the majority of the business turbulence encountered. But occasionally we are forced to fly into "severe" conditions.

Created by a team member's poor judgment and decisions, these workplace issues become a high source of stress and open the door for many other conflicts, including lawsuits. Often referred to as a "hostile" environment, your culture can be impacted greatly when a team member creates issues at work, especially if that team member is in a position of authority, like one of your supervisors.

Because most business environments employ people with different communication styles, personalities, backgrounds, and worldviews, conflicts can occur when they interact. These conflicts should never be ignored.

Below are issues that team members create, which will lead to severe turbulence. If any of these sound familiar, you must make evasive maneuvers and immediately resolve them.

Bullying	Gossip
Harassment	Discrimination
Theft	Disrespect

These issues do not happen by chance. They are made by choice and should fall under your list of "Non-Negotiable" behaviors. They cannot be accepted, tolerated, or ignored. From a military perspective, these issues could warrant an immediate discharge from service after a court martial.

If your flight encounters severe turbulence, you will not only need to enlist the counsel of HR, you may need to get your legal team involved. If you fail to address these issues, your legal team will certainly get involved, but much damage will have already occurred.

Pilot's Log:
Monitor any possible severe conditions, through direct communication with your team and leaders.

PILOT FATIGUE

Plain and simple, the true impact of business turbulence is exhaustion. Continually dealing with these hazards takes its toll on everyone, but mostly on the Business Aviators. Draining their energy, some experience fatigue, making bad decisions and losing credibility with their crew.

The International Civil Aviation Organization (ICAO) defines fatigue as "A physiological state of reduced mental or physical performance capability resulting from sleep loss or extended wakefulness, or workload." Pilot fatigue can lead to disastrous results.

When navigating through redundant and unnecessary business turbulence, Aviators place great risk on their crew and their flight plans. Tired business pilots may not have the stamina to reach their destinations, easily getting off course and falling short of their goals.

BAGGAGE CLAIM

Like most aircraft, an in-flight movie can be an added luxury, taking your mind off of the duration of the flight and providing some temporary entertainment. For your flight plan to be a success, you must be restrictive in the type of "films" allowed. Far too often, in most businesses, the in-flight movie is a drama, with issues from the beginning until the credits roll.

Your in-flight business movie needs to be an action movie, focused on taking actions from start to finish. As my daughter and her friends say, "Save the drama for your momma," and create a culture of action-oriented crew members. Your message is that drama will no longer be tolerated.

Even the smallest carry-on baggage can become a source of drag, weighing down your flight. But how do you transform the drama into action? Set expectations on behaviors to minimize the amount of turbulence you encounter. High expectations must be set for all, not just for some.

I am involved in some conflict resolution for nearly every client. Most have at least one "Sacred Cow," the untouchable person who reigns freely throughout the workplace, creating high levels of turbulence, but remaining uncorrected. They too, must be held to the same high standards.

I have spent time working with my clients to increase professionalism, reducing the impact of personal issues, and have sat in my fair share of warning reports and terminations for team members who created severe turbulence. To minimize the impact of intangible turbulence, Aviators must focus on four steps.

The Four Turbulence-Busting Steps:

1. Agree upon your non-negotiables

2. Quickly identify issues

3. Immediately implement solutions

4. Be consistent and fair

I have helped my clients to avoid turbulence by implementing the "two solutions for each issue" technique as well as putting time frames on issue discussions. One client in particular was constantly bombarded with team members stepping into her office to share issues about the company, other team members, vendors, and even clients.

Her environment had become a free-for-all of baggage; all dumped in her office. Once we looked at all of the time spent discussing the issue, we realized that many hours were being diverted from productive work. Also, the issues were not exactly issues, but more opinions.

She announced to her team, that she was reallocating her time to support their goals and the goals of the company, so team members were welcome to come to her office after 5:00 pm, off the clock, to share any issues that did not come with solutions. A total of 0 team member stayed after work to vent. That same quarter, their sales grew by 10%.

Pilot's Log:
Exhibit justice; you cannot afford to show favoritism on an elevating flight.

I probably should have turned on the "Fasten Seat Belt" light for this chapter because dealing with people and the issues they raise is never easy. But resolving them is always necessary for successful flights.

Congratulations for facing your issues head-on. It's time to pull back on the throttle and ascend to the next level.

Part IV

Ascension Enhancement

Aviation is proof that given, the will, we have the capacity to achieve the impossible.

~ Eddie Rickenbacker

Part IV

Ascension Enhancement

Geometric Elevation.

In 1903, Flyer 1 was piloted into the history books by Orville Wright, with his brother Wilbur running alongside. The first recorded flight was made the morning of December 17, at an altitude of... wait for it... only ten feet off the ground. Long thought to be impossible, once the goal of flight was accomplished, eager pilots began searching for new objectives.

We have come a long way since Flyer 1. Today, most corporate jets can fly at altitudes of 50,000 feet, with the highest certified altitude being held by the Concorde at 60,000 feet. But there is a huge difference between ten feet up and ten miles up. Like most business pilots who achieve consistent flight, you may have the desire to ascend even higher, experiencing geometric elevation by taking your business to exciting new levels of growth.

You are well on your way to higher elevation and success by mastering the first three Forces of Business Flight. The unique combination of designing your flight plans, developing your Flight Crew, and learning tactical maneuvers have positioned you for high levels of organic growth. To achieve the higher ascension of your full vision, you must make enhancements to strengthen your aircraft and crew.

In aviation, each aircraft receives a certified maximum altitude. Test flights set the appropriate safe flight level a plane can maintain, but also identifies the maximum altitude, should it have cause to ascend beyond that limit. To reach new levels in business, you will also need to accurately test the limits of your aircraft and your crew.

Most importantly, you will test your skills as a Business Aviator. Can you pilot your company to new destinations by ascending even higher? As you can imagine, reaching new altitudes is not always easy. Statistics show that only one in ten companies succeed in achieving sustained, profitable growth.

To achieve your vision, you and your leaders must identify the measure of your organization's success. Elevation can be achieved by increasing your top line revenue or improving bottom line profitability, resulting in organic growth. But exponential business growth can translate into new locations, new team members, and new offerings. Business pilots can achieve ascension in a variety of arenas.

Types of Exponential Business Growth:

New Markets	Mergers
New Products	Acquisitions
New Services	Partnerships
Franchising	Licensing of Intellectual Property

All of these are viable ways to ascend higher; to achieve growth at faster rates. But anxious business pilots often adjust course, prematurely, and attempt to reach these new levels without enough planning. Many experience disastrous results. Having the desire to soar higher is commendable, but should be pursued with great diligence.

At the media company, we focused exclusively on organic growth for the first three years of elevation. But we had the desire to test the limits of our aircraft and ascend higher. We eventually adjusted our Flight Plan to include new markets, such as developing clients in New York and Europe, and we hired new, high-level team members. Our new services included high definition and editorial, and we acquired some smaller businesses.

Each type of exponential business growth presented a vast array of opportunities, but also put our flight in the direct path of new challenges. Ascension that occurs prematurely can come with a price, taking a heavy toll on the business aircraft and Flight Crew. Before pulling back on the throttle, be aware of the issues associated with exponential growth.

EXPONENTIAL GROWTH ISSUES

There may be nothing as scary as witnessing the oxygen masks drop down during your flight. It is a direct signal that something went wrong. But when you're five miles up, there is little you can do, except to put the mask on and hope the pilots have everything under control. A rapidly elevating business can experience similar concerns.

You and your crew have dedicated time, energy, and resources to successfully take off and *ELEVATE*, by focusing primarily on organic growth. But exponential growth often presents new challenges to Business Aviators, requiring important decisions to be made. The ill-prepared business Aviators can quickly become overwhelmed and lose focus.

When opportunities for exponential growth present themselves, be aware of the issues that your flight may encounter, related to the new, higher levels of ascension. Controlling the challenges can seem daunting, unless you understand them and plan accordingly.

Growth Issues:

Insufficient Infrastructure	Customer Service
Inexperienced Crew	Disagreements

Insufficient Infrastructure: Growth can test the operational end of a business, placing additional stress on the systems already in place. Due diligence and long range flight planning will relieve much of the problems as you and your crew prepare for the additional workload associated with business expansion. Your Organizational Charts and Job Descriptions will need to be adjusted to account for the new responsibilities and duties associated with growth.

Inexperienced Crew: If your crew is not skilled in maintaining flight with these new types of growth, their lack of experience can translate into frustrations. Your flight plan may require new team members to come on board, with the experience necessary for ascension. But you may also need to allocate specific training to your existing crew members to enable and empower them to perform the new duties required of their positions.

Customer Service: Achieving new levels of elevation is a sign that your customer service is also at high levels. It has been a priority as you grow, but ironically, it is one of the first things that tends to fall from the sky when business growth happens too rapidly. Your enhanced Flight Plan must maintain the high satisfaction that your customers have come to expect from your company and your team.

Disagreements: Business Aviators must all be on the same page with rapid growth. The cohesion of the key leaders can become problematic if disagreements go unresolved. Get everyone on the same page and make the necessary adjustments to your Flight Plan, before ascending at a higher angle. Do not let opportunities of growth create intangible turbulence.

Other problems, such as lack of capital and market fluctuations, can also negatively impact your ability to grow. Exponential growth issues are not issues if properly planned for. They provide you and your crew the ability to up your game. If you are not prepared, these issues will have a significant impact on your entire crew, causing your "oxygen masks" to drop.

CHANGE NOTHING - ENHANCE EVERYTHING

No one likes change, but everyone likes enhancements. One of the most important perceptions I immediately enhance is the perception of change. Working with my clients, I change nothing, but together, we enhance everything, creating an environment that faces challenges head-on, preparing the crew for new opportunities.

I have enhanced leadership teams, sales systems, and workflows. Did things change? They enhanced! But I never begin with, "I want to change your entire sales system." Instead, I always lead with, "Let's enhance your entire sales system," because exponential growth requires enhancements.

Since the first flight, aircraft have been in a constant state of enhancement, not change. Issues have been encountered and solutions have been identified, allowing aircraft to achieve new levels of flight. One of the most significant enhancements in aviation came in the way of flight rules.

The FAA establishes the rules and regulations to govern flight. There are two sets of rules for flying aircraft: VFR (Visual Flight Rules) and IFR (Instrument Flight Rules). Some conditions allow for visual references, while others require the use of instruments to fly safely.

Operating an aircraft under VFR is simple, referring to flying in clear conditions. Pilots can reference outside visual cues to maintain their orientation. To achieve elevation and safe "separation" from other obstacles, they may use nearby buildings, the terrain, and even the horizon for navigation.

To fly under IFR, a pilot must be certified, having an instrument rating. This allows pilots to fly longer distances, at higher altitudes, at night, and during bad weather conditions. IFR pilots rely on their Flight Crew and support crew, such as air traffic control, for additional viewpoints and guidance. A VFR-only rated pilot is not authorized to fly IFR.

Exponential growth opportunities occur as your aircraft consistently elevates. But too often, VFR rated Business Pilots attempt ascension without any certification; enhancements. When not equipped for IFR levels of growth, they jeopardize their flights. By focusing on three key elements, you will make the enhancements needed for ascension.

The Three Elements of Ascension Enhancement:

1. Structural Integrity

2. Re-fueling

3. Breaking through the Atmosphere

Chapter 9

Structural Integrity

Holding it ALL Together.

There is a reason why Wilbur Wright was able to run alongside his brother, Orville, during his first flight. Flyer 1 flew for 12 seconds and maxed out at a speed of only 6.8 miles per hour. 44 years later, pilot Charles "Chuck" Yeager would enter the history books for another record. On October 14, 1947, flying the rocket-powered Bell XS-1, Yeager broke the sound barrier.

At an altitude of 45,000 feet, he achieved Mach 1.07, traveling at an incredible speed 768 mph. The X-1 he flew that day is now on permanent display at the Smithsonian Institution's National Air and Space Museum. Of course, new questions about the limits of speed and altitude continued as pilots asked, "How fast and how high can we go?"

These questions led to structural designs, which supported the new aviation goals. So, how fast and how high have we flown? The X-15 set new records by reaching the edge of outer space (over 50 miles up), and achieved Mach 6.72, traveling an unbelievable speed of 4,520 miles per hour.

Flyer 1 was not equipped for that type of flight. It did not possess the structural integrity to keep the aircraft together through those levels of speed and ascension. Most businesses need to enhance their structural integrity to match their lofty elevation goals.

In aviation, aircraft flying at high speeds and high altitudes are subject to dangerous levels of stress. To minimize the impact of this pressure and ensure a safe flight, engineers focus on design enhancements before the ascension is attempted. For businesses, adjustments in their structural integrity will allow for higher, sustainable levels of growth.

PREPARING FOR ASCENSION

At the media company, we kicked off 2004 with a 90-Day Flight Plan that unified and energized our crew. By linking together back-to-back 90-Day Flight Plans for the entire year, we elevated to 23.99% sales growth from 2003. As you can imagine, we were excited to repeat the process.

Again, our consistent 90-Day Flight Plans helped us to reach new levels of success. In 2005 we grew by over 50% in sales results. This growth was organic, as we fine-tuned our sales system and developed our sales crew. We also began to open new windows of opportunity.

To maintain the highest levels of customer satisfaction, we had already begun to make some enhancements to our aircraft, like extending our operating hours. Originally open from 9:00 am to 7:00 pm, we opened a couple of hours earlier and stayed open a few hours later. We adjusted our shifts accordingly and trained our staff to handle the extended time periods.

It was not long until we had three shifts: day, night, and graveyard. Our focus on elevation was paying off and we were earning the business of many new clients as our crew worked around the clock. As the vice president, I also led our sales department, stepping into the pilot's seat to maintain our elevation, and I focused on developing my own new clients.

It had been years since my film school days at USC, but I was reconnected with a college friend who was now an editor at South Park, which was the number one show for Comedy Central. I went to visit him at their studio and was introduced to the Post Production Supervisor.

Watching their crew put the show together was an amazing experience. As we began providing media services for each of their episodes, we made some minor adjustments to account for their short turnaround times. But the media industry was about to go through a huge transition that would cause us to make major internal enhancements: high definition.

Moving from standard definition to high definition was not an option if we wanted to stay in business. It was federally mandated and the new high definition services certainly qualified as exponential business growth. But with it came a wave of challenges.

We required new equipment, which was costly. We needed a crew that could accurately run the jobs on the equipment, even though everyone in our industry was at the beginning stages. We required new tape stock and had to prepare for the inevitable learning curve. Our clients needed us to have all of the answers at a time when there were mainly questions.

With our past flight plan successes, we were dedicated to ascension; to geometric elevation. We made the commitment to South Park and to support their transition to high definition. Our crowning moment came on March 11, 2009 when South Park aired their thirteenth season premiere, episode 182. "The Ring" was their first episode to be broadcast in high-definition. My crew was involved in that process.

With high definition, there were many more variables than standard definition. The set up times were longer and the amount of media data increased significantly. We expanded our storage drives and band width to account for more data.

Many months of planning, testing, and enhancements positioned us to become a premiere high definition post-production facility. Wow, what a mouthful. But we ascended to new heights by ensuring that our aircraft and our crew could handle the new pressures.

As we began to comfortably fly at new levels, the business growth we experienced from adding this new service opened up additional opportunities. We would soon expand our services to include full editorial capabilities as we started to prepare for opening up another location.

There were ample opportunities for us to fail; to stall in mid-flight. Undertaking a transition of this size was not easy, but we incorporated these growth opportunities into our flight plan and made every necessary enhancement to our structural integrity.

Pilot's Log:
Master your current Flight Plan to open up the opportunities to enhance future Flight Plans.

PREVENTING A STALL

Sitting in air traffic control school, I was taught hundreds of different concepts related to aviation. Everything from barometric pressure to weather conditions allowed us to have a better gauge on our role in flight support. But one concept fascinated me, both as a student, and as a passenger.

Our instructor described the "critical angle of attack," also known as the "stall angle of attack." The phenomenon can cause a plane to stall while attempting to elevate too rapidly. The *angle of attack* (minus the "critical") produces maximum lift coefficient. This helps the aircraft to *ELEVATE*.

The "critical" angle of attack, however, occurs when an aircraft ascends too steeply and stalls. This is not referring to the engines, but rather an aerodynamic stall as the wings stop producing lift.

Without getting too deep into the physics that cause this phenomenon, when the wings are tilted up too far, the air flowing over the top of them becomes disrupted and no longer flows smoothly. The plane will lose its lift and begin to fall from the sky.

As horrific as this sounds, I discovered that the solution is quite simple. Pilots are trained to angle the nose of their aircraft back down again and reestablish smooth airflow over the wings, again producing lift. When business pilots attempt to tilt up too much, too fast, they can also experience a stall, feeling like they are losing momentum as their aircraft drops.

As a business coach, this principle is even more relevant. I designed the BES to help you take off, *ELEVATE*, and ascend higher than you ever dreamed, eliminating the potential for stalls and dips in business. By developing the structural integrity of your aircraft, you and your crew will realize the true potential of your business and maintain the stability needed.

Structural Integrity:

1. Radio Communication

2. Workplace Design

3. Crew Schedules

RADIO COMMUNICATION

In the early stages of aviation, it was incorrectly assumed that the skies were so vast that two planes could never collide. Aviation communication has evolved over the years, adjusting for the new demands of flight. Each aircraft is equipped with specific devices, allowing pilots to communicate with their Flight Crew and any support crew involved with their aircraft.

Increased communication reduces the risk of accidents and has always been a crucial component to the successful functionality of aircraft movement, both on the ground and in the air. It is especially critical when new levels of flight are desired.

Initial techniques allowed ground crews to communicate with pilots by using visual aids such as hands signals and colored paddles. But pilots were unable to respond back. The invention of wireless telegraphy changed that, and Flight Crews could now send and receive messages in Morse Code from ground-to-air and vice-versa.

Radio technology was developed following the World War I, increasing the range and performance of aircraft communication. By the mid-1930s, the development of radar improved communication by tracking distance, direction, and speed of aircraft. This greatly improved air traffic control support.

In the 1970s, aircraft began to be equipped with computers, which led to to the development of a data communications system known as the Aircraft Communications Addressing and Reporting System (ACARS). In the mid 1980s the use of data-based communications became a reality.

Aircraft today use satellite technology to carry out voice and data communications. Safety has always been the primary focus of all communication enhancements in aviation, because communication issues can yield disastrous results.

The importance of communication makes sense in order to take off and *ELEVATE* your business, but as you strive for higher levels of exponential growth, crystal clear communication becomes paramount.

While entire books have been written on communication skills, one or both of the following basic communication issues can become dangers for Flight Crews:

1. Misleading Information

2. Lack of Information

When aviation pilots are misinformed, or do not receive the proper information, they can lose their spatial orientation, make critical mistakes, and unintentionally cause accidents. In business, reliable communication must always be established, especially for growth.

A stall in your business is typically the result of ongoing poor communication. As you ascend higher through new types of business growth, the transference of information must be on point. But for most organizations, communication is perhaps their greatest challenge, making ascension more difficult than it needs to be.

There can be too much communication or too little communication. How much do you need? You need enough to be effective. But what is effective communication? Effective communication eliminates the possibilities of errors. Communication can come in the form of one-on-one dialogue, group meetings, and accountability reports. But to be effective, and help with the ascension of your flight, it must meet three criteria:

1. Be Proactive

2. Be Relevant

3. Be Timely

Be Proactive: Far too much communication is reactionary, not allowing the person receiving it to take a proactive stance and achieve the desired results. Your entire Flight Crew must be committed to positioning their fellow crew members for success, providing insights that will allow course-corrections and improved follow through.

Be Relevant: Is there is too much commentary and not enough effective communication in your company. Remove as much of the personal opinions and ensure that professional information is translated: information that gets to the point and serves a purpose. Have an outcome and ensure that everyone uses crystal clear communication.

Be Timely: Information that arrives after the fact is virtually useless. "Watch out for the flock of birds in front of you," is not effective if it arrives after the bird strike. Crew members must be committed to getting the right information to the right people at the right time. Business ascension is highly dependant on timing.

While fulfilling the position of vice president, my team used a variety of communication tools: phones, walkie-talkies, e-mail, shift reports, etc. Regardless of the tool used, each one needed to meet the criteria above. Because many of our team members were providing vital communication to their colleagues on other shifts, a breakdown could easily occur. Did it occur? Yes, but we quickly resolved each issue.

A breakdown in the communication process may happen easily if the intended message is taken the wrong way. Even compliments can be perceived as insults and jokes may be interpreted as offensive.

As author Napoleon Hill once said, "Think twice before you speak, because your words and influence will plant the seed of either success or failure in the mind of another." Ineffective Communication can lead to unnecessary communication, distractions, and frustrations. None of which help to ascend and capitalize on new business opportunities. Aviators must monitor communication and hold their entire crew accountable.

Pilot's Log:
Elevate your expectations about effective communication in your organization.

WORKPLACE STRUCTURE

Small changes can often make huge differences. In aviation, an aircraft's aerodynamic quality is expressed as its lift-to-drag ratio. Over the years, gradual design enhancements have allowed aircraft to soar higher and faster, safely and effectively.

Structure significantly helps to hold things together. But not just structuring your business as a Sole Proprietorship or an S-Corporation. I am referring to the workplace structure that must be enhanced to support new levels of growth.

The structure of your business sets the hierarchy for the accountability needed to maintain high levels of communication. The manner in which your organizational structure is designed and enhanced will have a direct affect on ascension.

Sometimes, you will achieve GREAT levels of growth with minor design enhancements, not just major structural undertakings. While at the media company, we needed to physically build out part of our facility to add the five high definition editorial bays, most of our designs were tweaks to our systems and processes.

Without structure, redundancies become common, which will prohibit your Flight Plan from achieving the results you desire, causing your business stall. Structure allows team members to perform at the highest levels of efficiency to support your new business growth.

Workplace structure is best defined the way crew members, departments, and leaders collaborate within an organization to achieve ascension. Collaboration is critical to the innovative ideas needed to soar higher. Structure must be more than aesthetic; it must be functional, increasing your ability to ascend properly.

The structure of an aircraft can range from the design of the wings, engines, fuselage, and landing gear. In business, you will want to pay particular attention to enhancing the design of your company. Meetings, systems, production lines, and vendor agreements may need to be enhanced to handle the additional stress of flying higher.

CREW SCHEDULES

Ascension requires higher levels of communication, which places new demands on the design of your workplace structure; in particular to the schedules of your crew. Too many Business Aviators fail to make the adjustments needed to guarantee a maximum return on the efforts of their team as their company grows.

At the media company, we made modifications in our workplace structure to support our new Flight Plans and *ELEVATE* to GREAT new levels. New plans required new organizational charts, which required us to pay particular attention to how our crew invested their time. Because our company was eventually operating around the clock, crew schedules were critical for success.

Our directors supported the Flight Plan, our supervisors ran our checkpoints, and our specialists operated our stations. Each shift soon required a rotation of leaders and crew members to position each person for success, and to serve the greater purpose of our company.

In the military, the hierarchical structure, known as the Chain of Command, had a direct correlation as to how everyone invested their time to support the mission at hand. A functional workplace structure is tied together around specific schedules, allowing your team to perform their new duties. As your business flight ascends to experience growth from mergers, new markets, or new services, you can maximize time by scheduling your team for success. Everyone has a defined role to support your Flight Plan.

As we continued to grow, it became necessary to schedule meetings that would foster innovative ideas. Think Tank Meetings were launched, and key leaders focused on the solutions necessary for our new frontiers. Having a tight handle on our crew schedules allowed us to gain a better use of our time.

High speed and elevation can work when you and your team are prepared to enhance your communication, workplace structure, and crew schedules. Now, we will learn how to keep on flying with *In-Flight Refueling*.

Chapter 10

In-Flight Refueling

Do not Lose Momentum.

It was a hot summer day in August when a gunnery sergeant walked into base operations, stepping at a quick pace; as if any other pace was acceptable in the Marine Corps. He presented a unique opportunity to the Marines within earshot. A C-130 Hercules was preparing for take off and he asked if anyone wanted to go up. Without hesitation, I headed over to the flight line to board the cargo plane.

Watching aircraft take off and land from the perspective of the control tower was not as exciting as sitting in the aircraft as it sped down the runway. The pilot angled back and the plane lifted off. Within a few minutes we were cruising over the Yuma Desert, about 3,000 feet up. I may have been along for the ride, but the crew was on a mission.

From our altitude I could see for miles. Looking out one of the windows, I watched as two F-18 Hornets approached from below. As they elevated closer to our aircraft, a basket connected to a hose, slowly lowered from the C-130. Flying at about 250 mph, the Hornets engaged the small basket and began the process of in-flight refueling.

With precision and focus, the pilots of all three aircraft allowed for the successful transfer of fuel, enabling the fighter pilots to continue their mission without stopping. Once complete, the F-18s disengaged their connection with the fuel baskets. In unison, both aircraft banked to the left, dropped down about one thousand feet, then accelerated forward. Within seconds, they were out of sight.

For me, the flight was an exciting adrenaline rush. But it would take 15 years until I would discover the business tactic behind in-flight refueling.

AVIATION REFUELING

Immediately after the Wright Brothers' first flight, Aviators began to push the limits of an aircraft's capabilities. While striving to fly faster and higher, it became evident that there was a great benefit to remaining airborne longer. It costs time, energy, and money to frequently stop to refuel.

In the 1920s, Aviators began to experiment with aerial refueling. The first successful exchange of fuel, thanks to the enhancement made by Alexander P. de Seversky, occurred on June 27, 1923. Two slow-flying aircraft accomplished this objective. As they flew in formation, a hose ran down from a hand-held fuel tank on one aircraft and filled the tank of the other.

Over the past 100 years, new technologies have allowed for in-flight refueling at elevations of over 20,000 feet, and at speeds of over 300 mph. Needless to say, aerial refueling is not the first technique taught to new pilots. It takes skill and precision to perform this vital operation.

But the ability to refuel is paramount to military missions, allowing the receiving aircraft to remain airborne longer, extending its range. It also allows aircraft to take-off with a greater payload, by carrying less fuel. Additional weapons, cargo, and troops can be loaded into the aircraft without exceeding the maximum takeoff weight. Once airborne, the aircraft can top off their fuel capacity in-flight.

In combat zones, less fuel helps with take-offs requiring shorter runway lengths. Aerial refueling also reduces fuel consumption on long distance flights, with potential fuel savings ranging between 35-40%, which includes the tanker aircraft. So how long can an aircraft remain airborne?

In 1958, a Las Vegas hotel launched a publicity stunt with a Cessna 172 Skyhawk and a crew of two. Setting the world record for continuous manned flight, they remained airborne for 64 days, 22 hours, 19 minutes, and 5 seconds. In addition to aerial refueling, food and supplies were transferred to them from the top of a convertible Ford Thunderbird.

Not a publicity stunt, successful Business Aviators must enhance their aircraft, and their crew's skills, to enable in-flight refueling. Allowing momentum to end is not an option. Slow down to speed up, but never stop.

IN-FLIGHT REFUELING | 183

BUSINESS REFUELING

When you strive to accomplish important goals, time is of the essence. But preparing to *ELEVATE* to the next level can be problematic when your fuel gauge reads, "Empty". To achieve exponential growth, you cannot afford to land your aircraft to refuel.

Choosing to add new services, expanding into new territories, or initiating a merger, does not need to translate into a loss of elevation. But most business pilots often experience this type of "drag" when trying to grow in new areas.

Achieving high levels of elevation takes time and skill, but losing momentum can happen quickly. Just ask the business pilots who have mistakenly removed their hands from the wheel while "growing" their companies. Gravity quickly takes over and begins to pull their aircraft down.

While coming to a stop is a choice that pilots make, a better way exists. Are you interested in maintaining momentum and continuing to *ELEVATE* as you focus on new growth opportunities? Because you are reading this book, I am making the assumption that your answer is, "Yes."

Your entire crew must be trained to reliably handle the many different opportunities and circumstances that come with ascension, without losing altitude. The results possible from exponential growth come from a willingness to embrace the skills necessary for in-flight refueling. You and your crew no longer need to stop your flight to keep the engines running.

Refueling your business while it is in-flight will allow you and your team to continue to *ELEVATE* while experiencing growth. To develop and sustain a climate of business ascension, you will need to achieve in-flight refueling by focusing on three principles.

Business Refueling:

1. The Goal Formula
2. 3-Dimensional Sales
3. The Leadership Connection

THE GOAL FORMULA

Goals are an integral part of your Flight Plan. They are the vital steps that you and your crew will take to ensure the arrival at your destination. But when the decision is made to grow, to ascend higher, successful Aviators tap into the true potential of goals. Goals provide high levels of inspiration.

When I wrote my first book, *The GOAL Formula*, I did more than share the elements of goal-setting: the steps you take, in a specified block of time, with the support of the people you enlist to help. I wrote about the impact that identifying goals had on my wife when she was fighting for her life during her first bout with cancer.

As her caregiver, her oncologist encouraged me to keep her positive; to keep her spirits high. As they infused her body with chemotherapy, she said to me, "I feel like I'm going to die." As you can imagine, I was short on ideas to keep her positive. But one day, sitting at the side of her hospital bed, searching for anything that would give her a fighting edge, I said, "When you're not sick anymore, let's buy a house."

It was at that moment that I experienced the power of goals. Married for less than a year when she was diagnosed, we lived in a small apartment at the time of her cancer. But she sat up and began to describe our future home. She detailed the color of the walls, the type of furniture, and the plants we would have in our yards. I watched as the goal infused her with energy, re-fueling her in-"fight". Yes, in the fight of her life.

Not only did she survive her battle with Non-Hodgkin's Lymphoma, but she survived her next three bouts: basal cell cancer, breast cancer, and melanoma. During each new diagnosis, we harnessed the power of goals and set new ones.

In 2016, the chemotherapy caught up with Gina's heart. In front of me, she went into cardiac arrest, taking a final breath in my arms. I immediately started CPR and continued until the paramedics took over. They attempted to revive her by using a defibrillator. I remember clearly as the paramedic reached up and placed his fingers on her neck, saying, "No pulse."

I watched helplessly as they prepared for a second attempt. The defibrillator was charged and the command was given to, "Stand Back." Her body tightened up as the second jolt hit her. By the grace of God, her heart started again. She was placed in an induced coma and remained in the ICU for seven days. She was released from the hospital with an Implantable Cardioverter Defibrillator (ICD) in her chest. This was the most challenging incident we have encountered, and again we set new goals.

Business leaders often miss the opportunity to refuel, failing to tap into the power of their teams. Nothing motivates someone like their own important goals. At the media company, we certainly accomplished our corporate goals and ascended to over 300% growth. But I did not merely focus on the company objectives.

Our office was located in Santa Monica, California, an expensive area to live. No one could afford to buy a home there. The American Dream, owning your own home, seemed elusive. My crew's goals became my goals and I introduced many of our team members to real estate agents, loan officers, and credit repair specialists.

Our company became a vehicle for our team to reach their goals. Within the first few months of focusing on their personal goals, three team members bought their first-time homes. With our leadership team, we also focused on each team members' professional goals, doing everything in our power to position them for growth within our company.

By genuinely placing their goals as a priority, it was not uncommon for our team members to ask us what they could do to help with the current goals in the Flight Plan, as well as the new goals required for exponential growth.

Pilot's Log:
Goals provide the energy that will refuel your team with hope, drive, and inspiration.

3-DIMENSIONAL SALES

Because "sales" is the lifeblood (fuel) of your business, it makes sense to keep the stream flowing at all times. Unfortunately, many sales systems come to a screeching halt as businesses redirect to accomplish additional growth through new services, new locations, acquisitions, etc.

In my book, *3-D Sales*, I share that your sales machine is comprised of five interconnected gears: Prospecting, Contacting, Presenting, Set-Up, and Follow-Up. Ensuring that they continuously spin is essential. If one gear stops, the decrease in momentum will inevitably impact the functionality of the other gears.

In times of growth, sales people can easily get distracted, often becoming involved in the logistics of future growth, to the detriment of their present performance. While the input of your sales team may be valuable as you plan for new growth, and their training will be important as the new growth opportunities are implemented, organic growth cannot suffer.

But how can you refuel your sales machine while simultaneously functioning at higher levels? Just like a tanker providing the receiving aircraft with the fuel needed to travel farther, organizations that are striving for exponential elevation are best-served by enhancing two components to ensure sales ascension.

Sales Ascension:

1. Increase Referrals

2. Develop a Follow-Up Tool Kit

New growth requires time and effort, so you are wise to increase your sales results by increasing your ability to reap the benefits of multiples. Transforming your current customers into members of your sales team is an objective that will pay off tenfold. Increasing the level of the customer satisfaction you deliver will turn your clients into referral partners.

Everyone knows the importance of earning referrals, but the following statistics will encourage you to direct your efforts into developing a system for earning more.

Traditional selling typically yields about one new client out of twenty prospects. But referrals yield one new client out of six prospects referred to you. That increases your opportunity for success by 300%. Remember, at the media company, we achieved 300% growth, and referrals were a huge focus for our sales team. Satisfied customers send more referrals.

In addition, referrals tend to buy three times as much and stay with you four times longer. Most importantly, they are almost three times as likely to send you another referral. When you ascend higher, stack the deck in your favor and develop a system for tapping into the power of referrals.

One of the first steps to earning referrals is to send the message that it is good to do business with you. By focusing on Gear 5 - Follow-Up, you will increase their desire to send you new customers. But most sales people do not have the toolkit available to follow up at high levels.

When you see the statistics of proper follow up, you will divert energy to raising the bar for this gear.

Follow-Up Performance:
- 48% of sales professionals do not follow up
- 25% of sales professionals make a second contact and stop
- 12% of sales professionals make three contacts and stop
- 10% of sales professionals make more than three contacts

Most sales people do not follow up because they do not have a "touch" better than, "I was just calling to check in." To be effective at follow-up, you must have purpose. A toolkit of relevant follow-up steps must be clearly established and used with proper timelines. When follow-up is done right, the results speak for themselves.

Follow-Up Results:

- 2% of sales are made on the 1st contact

- 3% of sales are made on the 2nd contact

- 5% of sales are made on the 3rd contact

- 10% of sales are made on the 4th contact

- 80% of sales are made on the 5th to 12th contact

Most sales people miss out on 80% of their possible opportunities. With my clients, I help to develop their follow-up toolkit, identifying relevant touches that allow them to do more then check-in, it allows them to be relevant and memorable.

Your follow-up toolkit should include e-mail and phone touches that allow your sales team to share relevant articles, news events, company litera-ture, industry surveys, important videos, and anything else a client would find valuable. Each sales person needs to commit to twelve touch points, finding the right tools for each one. Refuel in-flight and further stack the deck in your favor, increasing referrals and follow-up simultaneously.

 Pilot's Log:
Transform each member of your sales team into 3-Dimen-sional Sales Leaders.

THE LEADERSHIP CONNECTION

You are now energizing your team with the power of important goals and you are powering your sales machine with more referrals and improved follow-up. Your refueling process is almost complete, but one final con-nection needs to be made; *The LEADERSHIP Connection.*

To ascend higher and achieve exponential growth, strong leadership is re-quired to hold the entire aircraft together. The Aviators will provide the spark necessary to ignite the fuel and provide the team with the addi-tional combustion needed to climb upward.

In aviation, refueling in-flight can present some obvious challenges, especially related to safety. Transferring highly flammable liquid may stand out as an obvious one. Another challenge is the skill set required for a successful operation. But the threat that most links to business refueling is the idea that the crew can become fatigued with increased flight time.

Growing a business does not conveniently happen between the hours of 9-5. Flight Plans that include geometric growth require an empowered, energized team. When a team fizzles, the plan fizzles. To experience continuous, exponential growth, leaders must infuse their teams with the extra energy (fuel) required for new levels of flight.

Most employees are not able to raise their own levels of motivation and inspiration. Two separate elements, some leaders confuse the two disciplines. When your aircraft ascends, you must ensure that your team has the motivation needed for short bursts of energy and the inspiration required for long-term success. That type of connection comes from their leaders. In my book, *The LEADERSHIP Connection*, I share concepts on making the link between leading and succeeding.

Providing regular motivational messages, leaders keep their teams going when others would stop. Motivation is like the half-time locker room pep talk to quickly realign the team with the task at hand. GREAT leaders provide timely motivation.

Providing consistent inspirational messages, leaders keep their teams focused on the destination. Inspiration is like the State of the Union Address that keeps the team focused on the long-range goals. GREAT leaders provide dynamic motivation.

Pilot's Log:

If earning a referral is the greatest compliment, position your company to receive more compliments.

Refueling is essential and your flight is now prepared to go higher and travel greater distances. But are you ready to make new breakthroughs and *Earn Your Business Flight Wings*?

Chapter 11

Earning Your Wings

Achieving Consistent Business Elevation.

On December 17, 1903, only one aircraft flew in the skies. A lot has changed since Orville and Wilbur earned their "wings" that morning. Now, more than 50,000 flights take off and *ELEVATE* each day, arriving at destinations around the world. To ensure safe and successful flights, the skills of Aviators, Flight Crews, and support staff must constantly be at the highest levels.

With the increase in aircraft activity, the Federal Aviation Administration (FAA) was formed on August 23, 1958. As the national aviation authority of the United States, the FAA regulates all aspects of civil aviation, including the construction and operation of airports, the management of air traffic, and most importantly, the certification of personnel.

To ensure that pilots continue to grow, the Legacy Program was created in 1996, offering a twenty-year recurrent training opportunity; twenty phases of skill enhancements. Each phase that was completed offered recognition; a set of wings and certifications acknowledging their status.

In 2007, the program became known as the FAA WINGS Pilot Proficiency Program, still providing recurring training for general aviation (GA) pilots. But it enhances the user experience and places additional focus on key safety issues.

At the core of the Wings program, activities are linked to the areas that pilots encounter the most struggles, including common errors, a lack of proficiency, and incorrect knowledge. WINGS credits expire after 12 months, unless one phase of basic training is completed. This ensures that pilots remain up-to-date and can safely command an aircraft on a regular basis.

BUSINESS FLIGHT WINGS

The purpose of the WINGS Program is straight forward: reduce the number of accidents. To increase the success of that objective, education and training opportunities are offered at three levels: Basic, Advanced, and Master.

Like an aircraft, your business was not designed and built for one single flight. The intention is that you achieve continuous, successful elevation by staying focused on your 90-Day Flight Plan and course-correcting, as required, to arrive at your destinations.

The BES is the business aviation authority, supporting Business Aviators and their flight plans by setting the protocols for progress. Identifying the enhancements needed in your company and providing tactical ways to achieve them, will help your crew to earn their business flight wings. Are you ready to earn your business flight wings?

In a corporate flight, earning your wings is crucial. Consistently sharpening your blade to provide successful flights at all levels is important. *ELEVATE* encourages business pilots and their crews to continually strive for enhancement; increased knowledge and results. Like the WINGS program, you can assess the performance of your Business Aviators and strive for new levels of success.

ELEVATE Flight Wings:

- **Basic** - 1 Flight completed
- **Advanced** - 3 Flights completed
- **Master** - 5 Flights completed

Basic Business Wings

Basic Business Wings are designed as recognition for Flight Crew members who have successfully participated in a 90-Day Flight Plan. Earning these wings (never given), a Flight Crew member has exhibited the highest levels of dedication, loyalty, and engagement. They did not go through the motions, but rather contributed to the success of the flight by having a sense of urgency during each of the 90 days. It is perfectly acceptable to not pin the wings on everyone from the flight, unless everyone earned them. Keep the expectations high.

Advanced Business Wings

Advanced Business Wings are designed as recognition for Flight Crew members who have successfully completed three 90-Day Flight Plans. Earning these wings, a Flight Crew member also exhibited the highest levels of leadership, setting the example to other crew members.

The Advanced Level is for Aviators who have elevated above the Basic Level. These crew members are typically in a leadership role and have begun to do more than carry out the Flight Plans, they have become instrumental in designing them.

Master Business Wings

Master Business Wings are designed as recognition for Flight Crew members who have successfully completed five 90-Day Flight Plans. Earning these wings, Business Aviators, do more than exhibit leadership, they develop more leaders within their crew.

The Master Level is for Aviators who elevated above the Advanced Level by developing new Aviators, and increasing the impact of the cockpit crew. They have begun to teach others how to pilot the aircraft so multiple Flight Plans can be developed and implemented.

At the Master Level, Aviators also focus on enhancing their support crew by developing key relationships with strategic partners; their suppliers, vendors, and colleagues who can provide additional support to their Flight Plans.

Pilot's Log:
The more wings that are earned, the more elevation occurs.

UFOS - UNDESIRABLE FRUSTRATING OCCURANCES

Look, up in the sky. It's a bird. No, it's a plane... that's off course, by yet another distraction. Business Aviators and their crews, even those who have earned their wings, can easily lose sight of their destination, when distractions block their vision. These Undesirable Frustrating Occurrences (UFOs) are too common, often during times of ascension,

In the aviation world, a UFO is described as any anomaly in the sky that is not identifiable. Of course, they are first thought to be visits from extraterrestrial life forms, which leads to countless theories of government conspiracy. Virtually all UFOs are later identified, most commonly being aircraft, balloons, clouds, or some astronomical object such as a meteor.

In business, undesirable distractions can come in all shapes and sizes. UFOs cause crew members to lose focus, looking busy, but not productive. Distractions at a company, are usually associated with employees getting off course to focus on something non-growth related: checking their social media sites, online shopping, or texting family and friends.

But those are small distractions in comparison to the UFOs that cause Aviators to steer away from the Flight Plan, leaving their core values, mission, and vision in their wake. The results of distracted Aviators can be devastating to the flight. So what could cause a business leader to lose focus?

Common UFOs that can Distract Aviators:

- Lack of confidence in the current market place
- The threat of new or existing competitors
- Personal issues at home
- Declining relationships with strategic partners
- Pressure from investors or board members to alter course
- New opportunities that are not in the current Flight Plan

Even during times of elevation, business pilots can experience any one or a combination of these UFOs. Uncorrected, the Flight Crew can become disengaged and forward progress can lose momentum. Identifying UFOs is the just the first step. To guard your business against flight distractions, cockpit communication must be at the highest levels.

Early in the morning on August 29, 2005, the Gulf Coast of the United States was struck by Hurricane Katrina. The impact was devastating, but the community tried to immediately rebuild. One technique was to offer movie studios tax credits on productions shooting in New Orleans.

Already on our Flight Plan, we were notified about this opportunity. If the film industry shot their movies in that region, they would need post production services, just like the ones we offered.

With no competition in a potentially exploding market, we could have easily been distracted, even while we were already elevating on our current Flight Plan. An Undesirable Frustrating Occurrence (UFO) could have been the result. But instead, the owner and I met with our Aviators and made the decision to explore the opportunity.

We planned a brief trip to New Orleans, which worked great for me as I love Cajun food and jazz. Our other Aviators assumed control of our current Flight Plan, and with constant personal communication, we made sure our flight stayed on course. Arriving in New Orleans we witnessed the devastating effects of the hurricane while also touring the area and identifying the potential of the opportunity.

We determined that the project did not fit into our current or future plans, so we aborted, before it became a distraction. We did not allow a UFO to get us off course. If it had panned out, we would have enhanced our Flight Plan and designed an alternate route.

Pilot's Log:
While UFOs typically turn out to be nothing, a distraction can turn out to be costly.

POST FLIGHT DEBRIEF

Landing an aircraft is typically considered the most dangerous part of flight. Speed is slower and more maneuvering is required as the amount of obstacles increase: buildings, other planes, and birds. According to Boeing statistical studies, "16% of fatal accidents occur during takeoff and initial climb, while 29% occur during the approach and landing." When interviewed, most pilots consider landing an aircraft the trickiest part.

As you begin your final descent and prepare your crew for landing (at your destination), it is not advisable to park your aircraft and walk away. After each 90-Day Flight, set up a time to meet with your team, discussing what worked well and what did not. Enjoy the successes of your flight, while planning for your next journey, as you hold a Post-Flight Debrief.

Just as aircraft are checked after each flight, it makes sense to examine your business aircraft; to find problems and have them fixed before you attempt to fly again. It also allows you to assess your crew, identifying their strengths and weaknesses.

A Post Flight Debrief is an essential part of the relationship-building process that will create a stronger crew for the next flight. Rewarding team members for their performance is an exciting part of this meeting, which helps to enhance buy-in for the next trip. Day 91 is an exciting time. Perhaps order in lunch and share successes as you award crew members with their "wings" and provide them the opportunity to share their experiences. It is also a perfect time to constructively review the lessons learned from the flight.

Have open dialogue about all aspects of the Flight Plan by requiring each crew member to complete, and share, their Post-Flight Checklist on the next page.

Pilot's Log:
All GREAT journeys begin with small steps, but end with GREAT strides.

E L E V A T E

Post-Flight Checklist

Gauge the status of your aircraft after your flight. Did you accomplish your three goals? Below that, rank the performance of crew and systems, using a scale of 1-5, 5 being best. Lastly, write down the unique challenges you encountered and the solutions for your next 90-Day Flight.

Goal #1 Accomplished	☐ Yes	☐ No
Goal #2 Accomplished	☐ Yes	☐ No
Goal #3 Accomplished	☐ Yes	☐ No

Crew - Teamwork	1 2 3 4 5
Flight Systems	1 2 3 4 5
Customer Satisfaction	1 2 3 4 5
Cockpit Communication	1 2 3 4 5

Challenges Encountered:

_____

_____

_____

Solutions for the next flight:

_____

_____

_____

THINK GREAT AND ELEVATE

When I became Gina's caregiver during her first battle with cancer, I shared a thought with her that we have used each day in our lives. In fact, it became a founding principle in our business and can become a driving force in your Flight Plan.

It did not take us long to figure out that there were only two destinations possible when fighting cancer: a clean bill of health or a funeral. That was a reality that we faced as soon as her oncologist confirmed, "You have cancer."

Once the treatment plan was laid out in front of us, I remember sitting with Gina in our apartment, as we quietly pondered the journey ahead. Seven cycles of chemotherapy, a month of radiation, and a stem cell transplant were all part of her route over the next year.

The thought came to me after her oncologist encouraged me to keep her spirits high. He mentioned that a positive attitude would help her to fight back. So I held Gina's hand and said, "We are going from Point A to Point B. We don't know how long it will take to get there or what every challenge will look like. We do not even know exactly where we will end up. But we are going to go there together, with our best foot forward."

In 1999, Gina and I made the decision to think differently about our journey as a cancer patient and a caregiver. We chose to embrace the opportunities in front of us and not to succumb to our circumstances. In 2008, we took that same mindset and started our business, Think GREAT. We had the desire to help people to think differently about their challenges and accomplish their goals, no matter what circumstances they face.

As you *ELEVATE* from Point A to Point B, you will accomplish much more than your goals. I remember elevating to 300% growth at the media company. Our destination was always an important focal point for our team. But the greatest reward was the bond that occurred when a group of people became a team; a GREAT team focused on new levels of success. We celebrated each victory and learned from each defeat.

Most importantly, our desire to succeed translated into an opportunity for personal and professional growth because we made the decision to go from Point A to Point B with the best possible attitudes. While we may have enhanced our business, it was the ability to transform our crew that provided the greatest feelings of accomplishment for all of us.

As you guide your aircraft into the heavens, always remember to Think GREAT as you *ELEVATE*. Enhance the perceptions of your crew and lead them to new destinations - personally and professionally. Guide your crew from Point A to Point B, at the highest levels of engagement and excitement.

Think GREAT and *ELEVATE* to new and exciting levels!

ACKNOWLEDGMENTS

My Deepest Gratitude

This book would never have taken flight without the support of the following people. I am eternally grateful for the impact you have made in my business; in my life.

Gina, we have certainly experienced some crazy turbulence on our flight together. Through it all, your inner strength, and your belief in me, has pushed me to new levels. You are more than my co-pilot; you are truly my best friend.

To Erika, my passionately dedicated daughter - you sacrificed so much time with me, allowing me to work on this book when we could have been playing. You also helped, as my Executive Assistant, with anything I needed.

To Sandy Crosby, you are much more than my Director of Business Development, and my sister-in-law, you are an integral part of the Think GREAT Team. Your dedication and passion to our company and to our clients, has helped Think GREAT to *ELEVATE* to incredible new heights.

To Brooke Zahn, your professional and heartfelt suggestions were much more than mere editing. Your insights and contributions took *ELEVATE* to the next level and transformed this book into a powerful business resource. You are amazing!

To my clients, for your unwavering trust in me and the concepts in this book. Together, we have been on an incredible journey of elevation. You have opened your doors and welcomed me into your businesses as an extension of your team and for that, I am beyond appreciative.

About the Author

Erik Therwanger

Erik Therwanger began his unique career by serving in the U.S. Marine Corps. Leadership, honor, and integrity did not end after his four year tour of duty; they became the foundation of his life, both personally and professionally.

After receiving the news that his wife had been diagnosed with cancer, Erik left his job in the entertainment industry, became her caregiver, and started his new career in sales. With no formal training, he began selling financial services. Relying on the strategies and techniques he learned as a Marine, he quickly became a top producer, recruiter, and trainer.

Erik's passion for helping others to accomplish their goals led to the creation of Think GREAT®. He successfully blends his leadership skills, his unparalleled ability to inspire and develop teams, and his wide array of sales experience, to provide practical solutions for individuals and organizations.

Sharing his personal story and elite strategies, Erik inspires audiences to strive for new levels of greatness. His interactive and powerful workshops highlight his step-by-step process for increasing results: The Business Elevation System (BES)™. Erik delivers a compelling message that leaves a lasting impact in organizations, creating the necessary momentum to develop strong leaders, build visionary teams, and *ELEVATE* sales results.

As the author of the Think GREAT® Collection, Erik has combined his challenging life experiences with his goal–setting techniques to provide proven strategies to enhance the lives of others.

As part of his greater purpose, Erik dedicates time to helping in the fight against cancer by volunteering with the Relay For Life. Erik is also a member of the Marine Corps League and Beyond the Yellow Ribbon, participating in events to support our nation's veterans and their families.

www.ThinkGreat90.com

Please visit our website for additional information to help you and your organization achieve greater results:

- Powerful Products
- Inspirational Seminars
- Interactive Tools
- Events and Appearances with Erik Therwanger
- Register for the free GREAT Thought of the Week

For additional information, please visit
http://www.thinkgreat90.com

Additional books in

- *The LEADERSHIP Connection*
- *The GOAL Formula*
- *3–D Sales*
- *The SCALE Factor*
- *Goal Planning Strategy (G.P.S.) Workbook*

Made in the USA
Lexington, KY
25 March 2017